FOOLED AND FAILED GENERATON

WAKING UP AND SAVING AMERICA

Conversation with Young Voters

JAMES M. ADAMS

DEDICATION

This book is dedicated to my Mother and Father.

CONTENTS

INTRODUCTION

In 2008, American youth elected Barack Obama as President of the United States hoping to enjoy a young president who represents their generation. Indeed, many young people were excited to elect someone who is young, good-looking, articulate, and energetic who promised a worry free life. Unfortunately some young people always appreciate whatever is cool and whatever is gained effortlessly.

Parents put forth a lot of effort to provide their kids with everything they want to make sure that their life at home was complete joy. Most kids do not even help parents with little house work such as mowing the lawn, fixing broken stuff, cleaning, preparing food... They in many cases do not clean and keep in order their own bedrooms. Engaged with electronic devices, they do not have any idea what is going on around them. They do not talk to parents about anything. They are completely cut off from the external world. They have their universal world inside those electronic devices and with a few friends. Politics is the last thing on their mind. When they reach eighteen, suddenly they start making big political decisions to elect officials for high positions without understanding their choices and consequences.

There are some young people who are eager to understand the country, politics, and economic problems in their high school years. However, their number is limited. The majority of high school graduates do not understand all these issues. They go to college and enter the workforce without any clear idea about politics and governmental policies. One picks an engineering major in college but has no idea what would be the impact of politics and the economy on engineering work. Everything is rosy and great when you open your eyes. When these kids mature at work, they understand in order for them to succeed in their profession, the country has to be a good place to work and live. It can be so only if economic policies of the government facilitate high economic growth and prosperity. Policies of the government may impede or support economic prosperity.

Unfortunately, policies of President Obama impede economic growth. Therefore, unemployment rates are high, economic growth rates are low, and the U.S. is losing the competition with other nations. Those young people who voted for Barack Obama did not understand the whole complexity of the situation in 2008. Electing an inexperienced person as U.S. President at that horrible economic crisis was a tremendous failure of voters, specifically young voters who were under a false impression.

Young people listened to Barack Obama who promised to fix the economy soon. They did not have a better choice. Senator McCain was not articulate and was not able to explain clearly what measures he would take to get the country out of the mess. However, McCain had many years of experience and might have turned the country around with his team that he might have been able to create because he had an extensive network of highly competent people. He was not Bush as he said. However, this did not help. Young people were confused by Senator McCain's position who promised something for the military and veterans, but nothing to others. Barack Obama promised everything to everybody even though he did not know how he would keep these promises.

The main concern among the older generation was Obama's background experience. It was clear from the beginning that he did not possess any executive experience in business or public office. He did not manage even a small group of people, and never administered a payroll. He never had managerial experience. He was a two-term state senator and had been a U.S. senator for two years, most of which he spent campaigning. However, he had an ideological platform based on social justice. He viewed the U.S. as an unjust society that had very rich and very poor citizens (by international measures, poor people in the U.S. are classified as rich). Therefore, he believed that the government has to redistribute wealth through additional governmental programs and taxation policies as in Western Europe (which is in deep social crisis: not able to fund their monstrous social programs) and the former communist nations.

Today's questions are the following:

Was it reasonable to go with another welfare program in the middle of a deep recession?

Is it reasonable to take wealth from the rich and give to the poor, killing any incentive among the poor to provide for themselves and among the rich to succeed?

Would it not fundamentally change the American way of capitalism?

Would it not kill incredibly high individual motivation that made America great?

Are there any other ways to make poor people better off?

In fact, poor people have a safety net in the form of food stamps, Medicaid, and earned income credits, and are not obligated to pay federal and state taxes.

Obama's efforts are about redistributing the wealth of the rich among not very poor people, making eligible for Medicaid millions of uninsured citizens who chose not to buy health insurance and spend their money to buy something else. In other words, people who are not so poor but do not want to purchase insurance will be automatically enrolled into Medicaid by the Affordable Health Care Act or Obamacare that the country cannot afford in the middle of a recession.

President Obama's policies are in their entirety more politically motivated than economically reasonable because they are focused on the voter base in the next presidential election. All of his polices such as Obmacare, green energy projects, and financial regulation are not reasonable in the middle of a deep recession because they increase governmental spending while tax revenues stay low, restrict production of traditional energy (oil), and limit banks' abilities to lend. Most importantly, these policies destroy the fundamental principles of capitalism. Thus, they destroy the mechanism that creates wealth for people and the country and makes the U.S. the most powerful and exceptional country in the world.

Many young people are opportunity seekers and want America to remain the land of opportunities. However, America has stopped being so since Barak Obama took office in 2008. They voted for Obama because they overestimated or did not evaluate his abilities at all.

In this book, I explain in simple words why young voters are so confused and do not make thoughtful decisions on such a critical and fundamental issue as hiring the President and members of Congress and local officials. I will also explain in simple words President Obama's ineffective policies for this country (soft hits – poor economic policies: he did not have any hard hits except killing Osama Bin Laden) and cheap shots: je broadened his voter base by abusing his executive power. I also suggest ways how America can be saved waking up on time and becoming unique and great again.

PART I

FOOLED AND FAILED GENERATION

Chapter 1
Financial and economic crises

Most young people did not have any understanding of the financial and economic crisis in 2008. In most families parents continued to provide them with anything they wanted. Those families that had hardship in that year because of job losses tried not to explain to their kids what happened or kids did not ask why bad things were happening. Unfortunately those bad days did not go away. Economic recovery has not happened. Young people must understand the basics of the financial and economic crisis to make right decisions on who might be able to handle complex situations without any ideological predispositions.

The financial crisis occurred as a bubble on September 10 of 2008, right after Barack Obama's primary victory over Hilary Clinton became evident and it also was clear that the next president would be Barack Obama because Republicans were about to nominate John McCain, who always supported President Bush, who conducted the unnecessary Iraq war. Therefore, Obama had an advantage. The Iraq and Afghan wars had a devastating impact on the American economy. If Senator Clinton had won the Democratic primaries, the financial crisis might not have irrupted because domestic and international investors perceived Obama as an inexperienced politician. Stock prices fell significantly before and after Obama's victory and investors lost about half of their wealth. The Dow Jones industrial average of the 30 largest U.S. companies fell from 14,165 points on October 19 of 2007 to 7,553 points on November 20 of 2008. Obama's victory in the presidential election did not help stocks come back up.

On September 15, Lehman Brothers, a global financial services firm, went bankrupt because it lost over four billion dollars in profits. Then a chain reaction hit the mortgage companies Fannie May and Freddy Mac, and then other large banks and financial institutions were impacted by a domino effect. The government bailed out many of them, including the Bank of America and AIG. Additionally, the core of the U.S. economy, General Motors and Chrysler, were bailed out by injecting government funds into these companies.

As the financial institutions lost billions of dollars in panic in the stock market, they significantly reduced funding businesses. As so, businesses were not able to fund their operations, laying off hundreds of thousands of employees every month. This made mortgages go under water because the laid-off people were not able to pay their monthly mortgage. It is true that banks lent subprime mortgages in the past, providing mortgages to those who were financially vulnerable. They might not be able to pay monthly the mortgage at any time if something happened to the economy. However, I think Obama's advancement in the Democratic Party primaries was one of the factors that diminished investor confidence because the new president, unknown to the economic establishment, came from nowhere.

Young people had no idea how the financial crisis erupted and what would be the consequences if the country elected an unqualified president. Senator McCain was not highly qualified to be the chief executive of the country. There was no choice. However, Senator McCain had significant experience in the U.S. Senate, and the Republican Party almost always is consistent in its economic policies, relying on the philosophy of smaller government and the free enterprise system.

We always have crises, and the one that erupted at the beginning of the 1980s was deep also. The unemployment rate was over 10% when President Reagan took office. When President Obama took office, it was 7.8% and it went up to over 10% later. Based on Republicans' conservative approach, President Reagan was able to reduce the unemployment rate to 7% in three years. He did not impose any destructive programs in the middle of a recession such as health care reform. He did not impose any harsh regulations such has as the Dodd - Frank Act. He did not panic and cut taxes across the board. His policies worked and the taxpayer base became broader and tax
revenues increased, and deficit and debt decreased significantly.

Chapter 2
Excitement and the good life

Insofar as youth did not have any idea about the significance of the financial and economic crisis and its consequences and how it could be managed, they were excited about Obama, the least experienced candidate for president in U.S. history. Obama went to the presidency so early, not having enough tenure to be qualified. However, this did not bother the Democratic Party establishment that allowed him to run. The party did not check his background. The Party might have known about his background, but ignored because of the party's pathological liberalism that extends to irresponsibility. Obama was influenced by the communist ideology of Harvard professors that was in everyday use in the Soviet Union which went bankrupt because of the centralized redistribution of wealth.

Obama's narrative about hope and fundamental change ignited youth and not only young people who trusted him deeply and blindly. Indeed, his ideology was new for the United States but not new somewhere else. This ideology did not work in the communist countries and therefore they became stagnant - stopped growing. Therefore, they returned to the capitalist path. Why should we go the same way and then return as they did? Unfortunately, it is happening now.

Government never was able to provide a good life for people. This is illusion. Government can provide basic support to the poor and elderly, veterans, and the disabled. Every individual is responsible for his or her good life. Good life has to be earned if an individual is in good health. People elect governmental officials to make sure that they create favorable conditions for individuals to prosper through hard work. An entitlement society becomes stagnant as the communist countries became so. Their people expected from the government more and more benefits, making little or no individual effort for self-sufficiency and independence. Now many Western European countries are experiencing a great difficulty in funding their entitlement programs. Their economies are also stagnant. To win elections, political parties promise more and more entitlements and when business cycles (recessions, economic decline) come along, their promises break apart.

Government cannot limitlessly fund unreasonably increasing welfare programs, borrowing money from foreign countries and thus compromising the nation's economic independence and security. Governments' economic policies must prevent this. However, President Obama's policies facilitate dependency and discourage hard work, promising much in benefits (tax credits, free health care, unlimited unemployment benefits, free contraceptives...) to gain voter loyalty. I discuss these issues below in other chapters.

Chapter 3
Disconnect

Young people are engaged in their own world. Parent - child connections are being lost. Kids all day long are with electronic devices listening to music, playing games, and communicating with one another. Parental wisdom is not being transferred to their kids: there is a huge misunderstanding among them. Most parents know what is going on around them, in the country, politics, and economy. They can be good advisors for their kids in making right decisions. However, this disconnect prevents young people from making right decisions on their own. Communicating over the social media with their friends who also have no idea about politics, the economy, and the country's problems, young voters make their own decisions. They wrongly assume that a young and good looking president who is armed with socialist and utopian ideas would create for them fun and a good life.

My son was excited to see Obama at his college speaking about hope and change. Now more matured, he understands that President Obama's policies were wrong for the capitalist country and contradictory to the idea of free enterprise, opportunity, and individual independence. In America, hope was always associated
with individual effort for prosperity, and change was associated with smaller government and more freedom. President Obama's hope is associated with governmental support of those who might easily support themselves if they make a little more effort. His change is about larger government, more governmental control over industries, more governmental involvement in manufacturing rather than in fundamental research (NASA is underfunded), more spending (he calls it "investment"), and naive assumption that the Muslim world can turn into democratic societies.

This disconnect with parents that lasted over kids' childhood results in misunderstanding important life issues when they start voting. They do not understand that electing a president is not a game or a gamble. It is a serious decision that will impact lives, not only their own, but their siblings', parents', grandparents', and friends'. If young people cannot find a job after graduation from college because of wrong policies that the president put forth, their parents, siblings, and friends cannot find better jobs to fulfill their aspirations and improve living standards. Even worse they may lose their jobs. Large and small companies still lay off employees from good jobs because of the declining economy.

Young people are not well prepared to understand politics and the country's economic and social problems. They do not communicate and discuss serious issues with parents, grandparents, teachers, and the older generation. Teachers at schools are mainly liberals under the hammer of unions and are often excited about Democrats voluntarily or involuntarily (unions push vote Democrat); professors at colleges do not discuss politics. If somebody does so, those are liberal professors who discuss far left ideology.

Managers on the work floor are interested in tasks, not in politics and do not educate their subordinates in politics. Young people do not watch television or listen to radio to get right information. Additionally, mainstream media are biased about President Obama and Democrats. Only FOX News, *The Wall Street Journal*, and a few other media outlets tell the truth about who President Obama is and what he is doing to the country.

Now, in the fall of 2012, college students are excited seeing Obama on their campuses, not understanding the scope of problems that he has created in the country. They continue trusting him, because they are hypnotized by the young smiling president's magic words about social justice through income redistribution. Social justice can be achieved through hard work by the individuals themselves. Government has to provide social justice to those who cannot provide for themselves due to health conditions and age. Young people have to open their eyes wide and clearly see what this country should look like: the land of opportunity or a nanny state? Mother Earth already had over a dozen nanny states which have collapsed because of the absence of any incentives to work. Hard work is building the Freedom Tower, hard work of Navy Seals killed Bin Laden, hard work built Chicago, and hard work built the International Space Station, hard work built your home, school, and the car you drive. Hard work made available smartphones and computers. Steve Jobs, Apple's CEO, paid the ultimate price to deliver to you iPhones, iPads, iPods, iMacs and other amazing things, disregarding his health conditions. He strongly disagreed with your decision to hire Obama as president.

China was a nanny state, and now it is turning itself into a capitalist country with the free enterprise system. European countries turned themselves into entitlement societies where people depend more on the government than being independent. Therefore, the economic crisis in the U.S. strongly affected Europe because reduced demand in the USA decreased the volume of imports from Europe. Recession hit many of those countries hard and entire countries were bailed out. There is no significant improvement in those hard-hit countries such as Greece, Italy, Spain, Portugal, Ireland, and some others.

Do you, young people in the United States, want that turmoil? Do you want to depend more on the government than on yourself? Instead of seeking opportunities, do you want to receive welfare from the government? Under Obama, many of you will not be able to find good jobs because good and the best companies are not hiring. They are waiting for good times after President Obama. Under Obama's policies good times will not come soon. The healthcare law, financial regulation, accounting practices regulation (adopted by President Bush, not repealed by President Obama) and other regulations restrict economic freedom for businesses. And so, they cannot expand, create more jobs, and hire you.

Young people vote having no clear idea what the elected individual would be able to deliver. Politicians talk great, sometimes hypnotize you, you will love them, and you get ready to vote for them. The reality is that some people talk great, smile beautifully, look cool but do not have any idea how their talking points would be implemented. Adults are not willing to dictate to their kids how to vote, youth is not willing to ask, and they vote blindly. In some cases adults are willing to tell their kids about politics, the economy, and the elections but youth is not willing to listen. The result is what we have now: massive debt, extremely slow economic recovery, high unemployment rates during the last three and a half years, and tens of millions of people are unemployed and underemployed. Additionally, because of wrong energy and economic policies of the Obama administration, gas and food prices are skyrocketing. People are of out of cash and do not have access to credit. Therefore, homes are not being sold and bought: the housing crisis is deepening; foreclosure rates are high.

Chapter 4
Blindfolded Democratic Party and voters

Young people and not only they were not interested in who Barak Obama was in the past. Even the Democratic Party did not do a background check. As I said, Obama did not have any experience in business and had only a little experience in politics. He was a community organizer in the South of Chicago, a two-term Illinois State Senator, and had two-year tenure in the U.S. Senate when he started campaigning for president. Having no experience whatsoever to be a president, he had a social-democratic ideology in his mind. That ideology never fitted the U.S. values and principles. The Social-democratic approach to politics in Europe restricts people's aspirations for greater opportunities and happiness. Heavy regulations and restrictions limit creativity, innovativeness, and commitment. Many people give up their aspirations because of heavy regulations of business. High tax rates (in France, it is 75% for the rich even though the wealthy there are not as rich as the wealthy in the U.S.) make businesses flee from the country. Many recent immigrants from Western Europe say that they came to the U.S. seeking opportunities because Europe does not provide them anymore.

Obama sent a message promising everything to everybody as he does now. People are mostly naive. They expect benefits today and tomorrow which bring short- term prosperity, but in the long run this prosperity turns into devastation. All the programs will be underfunded soon. The country is over $16 trillion in debt. Young people listened, and made blind decisions and trusted the presidency of the greatest and most complex country to the inexperienced community organizer.

Did young people know about how the country should be run? I do not think so. The President's obligations are to formulate a long-term vision for the country, put forth the right policies together with the Congress, and enforce them. The policies have to be focused on long-term prosperity rather than short-term benefits for voters. President Obama's vision was to provide short term benefits to voters who elected and would reelect him. People were excited about his vision. However, voters missed the main point, which was to worry about their own future and the future of their children and grandchildren. President Obama's vision was to redistribute existing wealth among voters now rather than strengthening economic power of the country which would bring long term prosperity. His vision was to keep people dependent on him in his first term so that they would be loyal to him in the next elections. Therefore, he restricted business activities, kept unemployment rates high, and provided welfare benefits by borrowing more and more money to please his voter base. Thus, over his first term he worked to widen his base by increasing poverty, the number of people on food stamps, and the number of people on Medicaid, and he increased the time an individual is eligible for unemployment benefits to two years. He did not take any measures on long-term economic recovery on purpose or did not know what to do.

Obviously, young people and not only they did not assume that he would fail. However, a little mature attitude might suggest that an inexperienced person would fail not only the presidency, but also a small organization. Voters were blind to this. Democrats voted for their candidates anyway even if their party was hijacked by people with social democratic aspirations. Non-Democrats voted for Obama blindly, not having any good idea about him and his background. Young people do not watch news, read newspapers, simply are not interested in politics. When it comes to making major political decisions, they blindly vote for those who are articulate and promise much. Youth must open their eyes and should educate themselves before making major political decisions.

Because of their blind votes, the country and people have lost their wealth worth of trillion of dollars and cannot get back on right track. The majority think that the country is headed in the wrong direction. When the turnout of young people is low in midterm congressional elections, the right people are elected. The high turnout of young people in the presidential elections of 2008 ended up with a disaster. Not understanding that young people would vote blindly again, the Obama campaign uses the social media to call them to go out and vote for Obama.

Chapter 5
Illusion about hope, change, and fundamental transformation

It was unclear what President Obama's change would look like. Hope: hopefully to end the deep financial and economic crises and have the economy growing again and facilitate creating more jobs? Or more welfare, more poverty, income redistribution, and free health care for many as promised? The second has happened. Change: possibly ending two wars without victory and any payback in terms of economic benefits and political loyalty? Taking over major private industries? Focusing on renewable energies and ignoring traditional ones and adopting an overwhelming healthcare program in the middle of the deep recession? Provoking Islamic revolutions in the Middle East, hoping they will get civilized overnight? In fact no hope has been delivered except putting an additional 15 million people on food stamps and letting children stay on their parents' health insurance until 26 years old, and providing unemployment benefits to the enormous number of people over two consecutive years. All the change has facilitated to the country's decline.

America has become great because of the system of free enterprise. Fundamental transformation was to limit economic freedom and charge higher taxes to those who create jobs, reinvesting their income, expanding businesses and operations. Another fundamental transformation was to turn America from an opportunity society into an entitlement and dependency society. The opportunity society means free market economy, free enterprise system, more good jobs, low unemployment rates; people earn their living and benefits by working hard and enjoying their jobs instead of collecting welfare from the government. The more people in poverty, the more people receive welfare and the more people appreciate President Obama. Being thankful, people eventually reelect Obama. This is the fundamental transformation that candidate Obama planned. This policy resembles policies of communist governments in the Soviet Union where people took more than gave to the society. Obama's fundamental transformation is associated with reducing the role of the United States in world affairs: giving up its world economic power-positions to China. Fundamental transformation is about being weak in foreign trade, importing significantly more and exporting significantly less and making the country's negative foreign trade balance even worse.

The "fundamental transformation" did not help return outsourced manufacturing jobs to the United States. Insourcing did not happen. Even more jobs were shipped overseas on the President's watch. Outsourcing jobs means that the number of outbound foreign investments is significantly higher than inbound foreign investments, which happened under President Obama's policies.

Green energy policy tremendously increased the cost of energy. The Environmental Protection Agency's Cap and Trade policy blocked new permits for oil exploration on federal lands and banned the Key Stone oil pipeline from Canada. The supply of traditional energy was significantly behind demand. Because of high-cost energy, all U.S. industries became stagnant. Many of them are in decline, especially tourism. Thus, no hope has been delivered: poverty rates have significantly increased; the number of people on food stamps increased by 15 million (from 31 to 46.6million), gas and food prices have skyrocketed. Change ended up with adopting the unpopular health care law, financial regulation, and a stimulus that did not work.

In terms of foreign policies, change provoked the Arab spring which ended up with the overtaking countries by Islamists. Fundamental transformation has ended up with turning the country from the land of opportunities into an entitlement society where more and more people have become dependent on the government, and citizens have become passive instead of being active opportunity seekers. Ironically, those growing passive dependents are the voter base for the President.

The dependency attitude of the citizens and helper attitude of the Obama administration buried the country with a little less than six trillion-dollar new debt in four years. It was an illusion that an inexperienced president who concentrated incompetent advisers around him (smart economic advisers resigned) would be able to deliver hope and change that fit the nation's value systems and to transform the country from a lower to a higher state in accordance with the capitalist free market principles. Instead, economic freedom has been restricted by the financial regulations and restraining energy policies.

The big change and transformation were the President's commitment to utopian social-capitalism and his ignoring any opposition or different opinions coming from the U.S. Congress which is responsible for laws and their correct enforcement by the office of the President. He announced that if the U.S. Congress did not let him do certain things that contradict the existing laws, he would do them on his own. He issued many executive orders that contradict or violate the existing laws adopted by lawmakers sent to Washington by their constituencies.

Chapter 6
Deception

President Obama talks well, but does not deliver what the country wants. Instead of being in his office to address everyday duties of the executive office, Obama has been campaigning all the years of his presidency mainly in the swing states. Obama's policies did not accelerate economic recovery after the recession. Instead they worsened the situation. If not for his policies, natural recovery might be faster. Capitalistic business cycles have this type of pattern. If there were no obstructionist financial and energy policies of the President, natural recovery might happen significantly earlier. The financial regulation and wrong energy policy as well as low confidence of businesses in President Obama made the recovery very slow. He is way off the values of this great country. This country's values are based on opportunity, individual freedom, hard work, and creativity. Therefore, this country became the economic and industrial engine of the globe in the 20 century. President Obama's values are based on dependency on the government and giving up freedom and opportunity as was the case in the failed communist countries.

President Obama's deception is about altering the country's values and pushing forward the ideology that discourages people from seeking opportunities and freedom. His financial regulations and energy policies put a great barrier in front of those who still seek opportunities. Now you cannot borrow money to create a small business. Even if you are able to create a business, energy costs make your products costly and non-competitive. You cannot sell, and you go bankrupt.

Liberal media understand all this but deliver false information about the President's deception. Collectivism did not work in the past, it is not working today, and it will not work in the future. Japanese collectivism ended up with a debt-to-gross domestic product ratio of 225%. The U.S. has a ratio of over 100%. It was 69.6 % when President Obama took office. This decreases the country's credit rating and borrowing from China and others will cost more. With low credit ratings, the country pays more interest on debt. Obama does not have any other solutions than borrowing.

Chapter 7
Euphoria and miscalculation

Very experienced presidents led the United States in the past. Voters always approached responsibly the task of electing presidents. So did political parties in nominating candidates. However, in 2008 youth said their big word coming out of their bedrooms after lengthy X-box or Play Station games to elect Barak Obama who resembled their videogame heroes, promising milk rivers and fruit-juice jelly banks. Indeed, playing games, young people never know the backgrounds of those characters that they play. Sometimes they pretend to be those characters. As youth get excited in the videogames, they get excited in elections. Facebook chats with Obama turned them crazy.

Euphoria had translated into votes. Indeed, Obama promised everything to everybody to get elected. However, he did not have any idea how he would keep his promises because all of them cost tremendous amounts of money. The economy was in the middle of a deep recession, and prospects of quick improvement were slim. He disregarded the crisis and did not try to fix it at all. Instead he imposed restrictions on corporate America, and businesses stalled, and stopped hiring people. This did not bother him. He continued borrowing money from China and others to fund his promised projects: green energy companies, unemployment benefits, food stamps, state governments, Obamacare, and transportation projects. These projects were not aimed at fixing the economy because they were not focused on job creation. They were focused on satisfying potential voters that would vote for him in the next presidential election. More about this you can read in the book.

Electronic gamers elected Obama and those who are still in college (seniors) do not realize what they have done to the country. Whoever is out of college has changed his or her mind about the President if he or she is not a committed Democrat. Whoever is in college now or works after graduation from high school is still confused and excited about President Obama. Now electronic gamers have to put off the game and wake up. Understand the country's problems that President Obama is not reporting to voters and make a right decision to fire him for poor performance. Remember, the country never had a slow recovery and then very close to a double dip recession since the great depression. The President's policies made it happen.

I think young people in this great country made a serious miscalculation (if they ever made any calculations) electing Obama in 2008. The country has lost an additional trillion dollars in GDP. Average household income decreased by more than four thousand dollars. People lost 40% of their wealth: real estate values decreased by this percentage.

Chapter 8
Unscrupulous choice

Changing presidents in the middle of a recession was a bad sign and it went against the slogan do not change horses in midstream. However, the country had to change presidents in midstream according to the Constitution. This change hurt much. All the policies of the previous President were altered except Bush's tax cuts. A new course for the country was taken from the far left (very liberal) position. Communists in the Soviet Union admired the leftist movements in America.

The Republican Party already had apparatus in place with eight years of experience. John McCain if elected might have fixed the economy within a much shorter time and he would not have moved from right-center to a leftist position even in theory. The new people in the White House and federal agencies with inexperienced president, advisors, and cabinet members were not able to manage the crisis and administered a stimulus package of over eight hundred billion dollars. The Senate and House of Representatives were in the hands of Democrats, but they did nothing to share their experience with the inexperienced executive branch of the government. Or the latter did not want to listen.

The White House actually had its own agenda to push Obamacare, stimulus, and financial regulation. The stimulus was thank you money to voters across the country. Most of the money went to state administrations to distribute among state-owned entities, mainly among teachers and other governmental employees. Part of the money went to unions and loyal businesses who contributed to Obama's campaign. This one-time spending drastically increased federal debt and consequently led to deterioration the country's credit rating. I will discuss the stimulus in detail in Part II.

The first negative impact of Obamacare is to mandate that small businesses purchase insurance for their employees that they never did before. They were stuck in the middle and stopped hiring new people. I will discuss Obamacare in Part II.

The financial regulation prohibits banks from lending money if borrowers do not meet strict requirements. So, businesses not being able to meet these requirements were out of money and continued laying off their employees. There was no chance to create new jobs by many of them. I will also discuss this issue in Part II. All those elements of Obamacare that have already been implemented are cheap shots. I will discuss this in part III.

Knowing all these failed policies I think that voters made a wrong choice in 2008. Obama campaigning around the country is not promising any change of this failed course. That indicates that the next four years of the Obama presidency, if he is reelected, will be catastrophic.

Chapter 9
Frustration (sorry about voting for Obama)

Many people who voted for Obama are frustrated because they are not better off. The job markets are tight. It is hard for college graduates to find good jobs. Many of them take jobs that do not match with their majors. Some other graduates after unsuccessful job searches decide to continue their education in hopes that they will get good jobs. Moms and dads at home suffer from pinching pennies because of high gas and food prices, hoping to save some money not for an annual but an occasional vacation in a few or many years.

The foreign tourism industry in the U.S. had below two percent annual growth rate over the last few years. Internal tourism has declined. The lodging industry has not reached the pre-crisis levels in its revenues. People cannot afford fuel costs in the first place. The routine route is work-home-work and occasional store visits. Fewer people go out to eat.

The food industry has declined. Not only customers but also businesses suffer from wrong economic and energy policies. The President's obsession with green energy in the middle of an economic recession and his ban on new oil exploration on federal lands and The Key Stone pipeline from Canada caused high oil prices. Consequently, transportation costs dramatically increased, and farm products that are produced using tractors that consume fossil fuel became much expensive and less competitive.

Demand for food has decreased because of high food prices as mentioned above. People put on their dining tables less and less food. Young people who are on their parents' budgets may not notice these problems, and parents to make their children happy may not tell them the whole truth. Even if they tell, they do not cut their support of their college kids who borrow more and more at higher and higher interest rates.

In many cases these kids do not care if their parents are struggling. Instead of understanding their parents, they escalate their commitment to their failed decision to elect Barack Obama. If kids did not suffer from President Obama's policies, their parents surely suffered badly. A bad life is coming if President Obama is reelected.

You may not be frustrated so far but your parents are very frustrated. More frustration is coming if you further trust President Obama's words that are ungrounded and impossible to implement because he did not do anything to reduce the nation's debt and deficit. His spending is out of control. He did not get his budget proposals in the Congress because all Democrats and all Republicans voted against them in all these three years.

PART II

PRESIDENT OBAMA'S ILL POLICIES
(SOFT HITS)

Chapter 1
Economy

Capitalist economy always develops in a cyclical pattern. However, in the 21st century deep recessions should not be possible, having high information technologies to predict and prevent. The consequences of every governmental action could be modeled and forecasted. It appears that nobody does so in the U.S. government as in Europe. They do not utilize findings of research and winners of the Nobel Prize in economics. Unfortunately, the new crisis was deeper than any other crisis since the great depression of the 1930s.

There were many reasons for this particular crisis. The number one reason is political. Each political party to please voters promised and then implemented programs that the country could not afford. In recessions tax revenues decrease and demand for governmental aid increases. The government covers the difference by borrowing money. Therefore, the nation's debt exceeds its gross domestic product (GDP) which is the market value of all officially recognized final goods and services produced within a year (quarter, month). The GDP is about $16 trillion and national debt is more than that.

President Carter initiated the 1977 Community Reinvestment Act (CRA), which compelled banks to make subprime loans to low-income borrowers. The housing bubble is the direct result of implementation of this Act. The main idea was to provide with mortgage (home loans) those who were not able to repay if they lose their job due to recession.

Clinton's administration adopted the welfare reform named "The Personal Responsibility and Work Opportunity Reconciliation Act of 1996 (PRWORA)" which added a workforce development component to welfare legislation, encouraging employment among the poor. However, the Obama administration waived this provision to several states so that unemployed people may not search for work and continue receiving unemployment benefits.

The last recession was unusually lengthy. When investor confidence falls because of wrong governmental decisions recession should last long. That happened in 2008-2012. Candidate Obama's rise and full absence of investor confidence in him and his associates and the future government caused panic in the stock and commodity markets in 2008 and 2009. Later we have learned that the panic was not groundless. Indeed, President Obama's policies did not make recovery reasonably positive. His policies imposed tremendous restrictions on economic growth because they prevented businesses from expansion.

Obamacare restricted new job creation because small businesses could not afford additional spending for health care. TARP (Troubled Asset Relief Program) was implemented wrongly, avoiding the normal bankruptcy procedures as laws require. Failed companies were bailed out; government provided them with cash instead of holding them accountable and forcing them to file for Chapter 11 bankruptcy protection as soon as possible. Precious time and money were wasted. The Dodd-Frank Wall Street Reform and Consumer Protection Act strongly restricted lending capabilities of banks, imposing significantly higher requirements for borrowing. This act made derivatives markets transparent, therefore killing this type of business which is fully consistent with the free market economy. It also made it impossible for families to buy homes, requiring large down payments and very high credit ratings. All these measures are holding back the economy from rapid recovery.

President Obama does not realize the content and consequences of his economic policies and is asking for four more years escalating his commitment to wrong policies. Because of these policies inconsistent with the free market economy, the country entered into a new prerecession in 2011. According to the U.S. Census Bureau's database, GDP growth rate was 2.4% in 2010, 1.8% in 2011, and 1.3% in the second quarter of 2012. Because of incompetent economic policies, over 23 million people in the workforce are unemployed and under-employed. Official unemployment rates remained over 8% over the last three years, and unofficial calculations suggest that it is over 11%, higher than it was when President Obama took office (7.8%). Because of high unemployment rates, demand in the economy remained low and therefore manufacturing grew at a very low rate. Service industries suffered from low demand also. Obama's focus on green energies made gas prices extremely high and consumers pay as much as twice for gas and have less money for anything else, producing less demand for other products and services.

The country is in decline and losing competition to whomever starting from China and ending with Vietnam in many areas of industrial production. Before Obama came to office, the country's overall competitiveness rating was one and now it is seven. Its credit rating has dropped to AA-. It was the highest, AAA, when President Obama took office. He promised to reduce the deficit (Deficit = governmental spending - tax revenues) by 50% from $438 billion in 2008 to $220 billion. Instead he more than doubled it and the deficit in 2012 was over $1.1 trillion. Is it not a disaster? The annual deficit is covered with borrowed money from domestic and international lenders. The annual deficit is equal to the annual debt.

The size of the federal debt increased by $5.4 trillion under the President's watch in 3.5 years while President Bush generated a little more than $4 trillion in debt in eight years running two wars.

President Obama spent the most money to fund entitlement programs because of increased poverty and sustained high rates (over 8%) of unemployment. The nation's debt ($16 trillion) now exceeds its gross domestic product. Gas prices have also doubled because of obstructionist energy policies. Food prices have dramatically increased. The price of beef has also doubled. Produce costs customers 50% more than two years ago. College tuition has increased dramatically. Overall, recovery from the last business cycle which is periodic and happens every 10 years was the slowest in the U.S. history because of restraining economic policies that prevented businesses from rapid recovery.

The U.S. economy is declining while the Chinese economy is growing at seven percent rate (if the Chinese government is not misleading). On the President's watch outward foreign direct investments (FDI) exceeded as much as double inward foreign investments. Outward FDI exceeded $300 billion annually. Obama's concept of job insourcing is not working. This is an example of the investment climate we had in these few years. The President blames Romney for job outsourcing, not acknowledging that under his watch because of his policies millions of jobs were outsourced to foreign countries.

The President's restrictive economic policies led to very slim economic growth because the more unemployed people, the less the demand. The higher the prices at stores because of high energy costs, the lower the demand. The lower the demand, the lower the production output and growth. This is gridlock. One of the main reasons is President Obama's green energy policies.

Chapter 2
Stimulus

President Bush initiated the TARP (Toxic Asset Recovery Program) to bail out (providing with cash failed companies that were obligated to pay back later) the auto industry and some financial institutions in order to keep them running. Congress approved over $700 billion for bailouts and Bush used half of it and Obama disbursed about $100 billion. If this bail-out money was supposed to be repaid to the government, President Obama's over $800 billion stimulus package (The American Recovery and Reinvestment ACT of 2009) was partly free money distributed among state governments and some favored businesses which made huge contributions to Obama's campaign.

In the U.S. Congress, only Democrats voted for it. In many cases states might be able to reduce their spending and overcome the crisis. However, the free money pouring from the federal government had been distributed among state-owned entities and was spent recklessly. The stimulus contributed to the $5.4 trillion additional federal debt generated by the Obama administration in three and half years. Remember, Bush added to the federal debt only $4 trillion in eight years. Most of the stimulus money went to the blue Democrat- controlled states. The stimulus funds went to some green energy companies and countless earmarks. Al Gore's company received over $500 million.

Chapter 3
Obamacare

The Affordable Health Care Act or Obamacare was drafted by the Democrat members of Congress behind closed doors and no Republican initiatives were incorporated. The law was adopted by Democrat votes only in both chambers of Congress. The law mandates every citizen to purchase health insurance starting from 2014. All the businesses small and large are obligated to provide health insurance to their employees and employees are mandated to buy insurance. Otherwise, organizations and individuals will be penalized in the form of an additional tax.

Another huge drawback is the expansion of Medicaid, which costs a tremendous amount of money and is impossible to implement because states cannot afford it as well as the federal government. However, the mandate may generate significant resources to fund the expanded Medicaid. States sued the federal government against Medicaid expansion and won the lawsuit in the U.S. Supreme Court. So, it is questionable if the program will be implemented as designed. Expanded Medicaid is being offered to those citizens who are not below the poverty line. The President is offering benefits in spite of the fact that people are not asking for them.

The law has some positive provisions: the elimination of the division of providers into in-network and out-of-network; young people may stay in their parents' health insurance plans until they are 26 years old; insurance companies cannot deny applicants based on their preexisting conditions; insurance plans are transferable across state lines. These provisions of the law are implementable without Obamacare's core provisions: mandate and Medicaid.

The health insurance system is being overtaken by United Healthcare, which is informally affiliated with the government, and AARP is its ally. It has already concluded expensive contracts with hospitals. If a visit (just being under the roof of a hospital, excluding procedures) to the emergency room cost under $300 recently, now it is over $900. Why? The Obama administration should answer this question. Low deductible health insurance premiums skyrocketed. Employees are highly "recommended" to buy high deductible insurance. Otherwise, both organizations and employees have to pay a penalty to the IRS in the form of a tax.

The Supreme Court upheld this law referring to the statement made by the administration that the penalty was a tax.

The Supreme Court does not recognize that Obamcare mandates people to buy insurance. The reality is that it is both a mandate and a tax. The law involves about twenty types of tax. The mandate contradicts the commerce clause of the U.S. Constitution.

Chapter 4
Financial Regulation

The main provision of The Wall Street Reform and Consumer Protection Act of 2010 named after Senator Dodd and Representative Frank who drafted the law is to restrict banks from lending money to clients that do not possess property, the value of which is not less than a certain percentage (in some cases not less than 60%) of the requested funds. It was around 30% in some cases in the past. So businesses are not able to borrow sufficient money to expand. This law obligates home buyers to make mandatory down payments, and credit scoring agencies must report to the Securities and Exchange Commission. The main purpose of the law is to control the financial system strictly.

The Dodd-Frank Act also requires transparent financial operations by investment banks and hedge funds, violating fundamental principles of commercial secrecy and confidentiality. If all the information is public, how would you capitalize on your ideas and core competencies? This law has a lot in common with the regulations in communist countries that eliminated any competition and made all corporate information public. In capitalism, firms have a right for their commercial information to be confidential. This fundamental principle is being taken away. Therefore, companies are not taking risk to succeed.

The law attempts to fight against everything that businesses do, assuming that they do wrong. The law was supposed to focus on the past decisions that created the housing bubble: chiefly President Carter's 1977 Community Reinvestment Act (CRA) that allowed selling subprime mortgages. The Dodd-Frank Act was supposed to obligate the executive branch of the government to take measures to avoid business cycles if possible. The law should have banned the Federal Reserve System's practices to artificially maintain high stock prices by reducing interest rates on governmental bonds. The Fed added air into the bubble.

Financial institutions and other companies are waiting for the political change in the country. Stock prices are increasing because stockholders are not willing to sell, awaiting regime change in the country, hoping a Republican White House will be business friendly. Remember, if businesses flourish, more good jobs will be created, and you will be able to take those jobs. President Obama's policies prevent businesses from creating good jobs. Almost all the jobs created in the last three years are very low-paying jobs. Most jobs were created in the states with republican governors: Texas, Ohio, Wisconsin, Virginia, and others.

Chapter 5
Green energy

The Bush administration started green energy projects mainly at the level of research and development when the economy was strong. Green or renewable energy sources are wind, hydro, solar, and bio fuels. However, their cost is significantly higher than traditional non-renewable sources such as oil and coal. Under Obama, over 200 coal-fired plants were closed and employees were laid off. Green energies cost 22 cents per kilowatt hour while coal-generated power costs 4 cents per kilowatt hour. The green projects consumed $22 in taxpayer money per kilowatt hour. Additionally, bio fuel projects made food prices extremely high. For example, the price of corn oil quadrupled since this project started. The use of corn for ethanol increased the price of livestock, consequently milk, products from milk, and meat. These projects are good only if they complement and gradually replace traditional sources of energy as they become readily available and price-competitive.

Implementation of green energy technologies in one country is not effective and efficient. Low-cost countries take over these industries as happened on President Obama's watch. Solyndra – a solar panel-producer - went bankrupt after losing competition to Chinese manufacturers. Some other companies funded by the Obama administration went bankrupt, wasting taxpayer money. The Obama administration purposefully banned new permits for oil exploration and drilling on federal lands and offshore. It also stopped the construction of the Key Stone Pipeline from Canada.

To promote green energies, President Obama discredited oil companies, not taking measures to shut the BP oil leak immediately. The military could have done so in no time. He let BP do so, which was not able to manage it. The BP oil spill in the Gulf of Mexico lasted 86 days causing a great environmental disaster. This served as justification to promote the green energy projects. If the President had let oil companies increase output, green energy companies might have gone bankrupt earlier. This energy policy held the rest of the economy hostage. The country lost a fortune. People lost jobs, homes, and wealth. Is it not frustrating?

The Obama administration did nothing to motivate the Organization of the Petroleum Exporting Countries (OPEC) to produce more oil. The President hopes that high oil prices will make green energy projects efficient. This provocative approach has already hurt the U.S. and European economies. Losses amount to trillions of dollars. Because of high gas prices, demand for other products, including automobiles, and services is lower than the prerecession levels. High energy prices contributed much to the cost of other products. Many products and services became unaffordable to consumers. Therefore, the economy is not growing. If it is still growing, it is only because of higher prices and inflation.

Chapter 6
Road and bridge construction

Roads and bridges are well maintained within the existing budgets. Some adjustments in those budgets are sufficient to satisfy maintenance requirements. However, President Obama decided that intensive road and bridge construction would create more jobs and resolve the problem of unemployment. After the Great Depression, President Roosevelt initiated extensive road and bridge construction in order to create jobs and jump start the economy. It indeed worked. Construction projects were mainly based on manual labor. Millions of jobs were created.

Obama decided to repeat this great strategy. However, he has not realized that roads and bridges have already been built and new road and bridge projects will not create millions of jobs because contemporary construction technology allows the use of minimum manual labor.

Therefore, it is a miscalculation. Other methods should be used. The best way always is to motivate private businesses that create jobs. As I said, private businesses are hostage to the unnecessary federal regulations and cannot create new jobs unless Obamacare is replaced, the Dodd- Frank Act is repealed and replaced, and production of traditional energy sources is increased.

I recently learned that President Obama wanted to build roads and bridges where they are not necessary. He wanted to have good roads in communities where he was community organizer. He simply could not find shortcuts or straight roads to those communities. Those communities had roads that were efficient to serve the needs of those communities. How can the country afford excessive roads and bridges where they are inefficient?

Chapter 7
Poverty

Slow recovery caused by President Obama's ineffective economic policies facilitates the increase in the number of people who live below the poverty line. If in 2008 there were 39.8 million people living below the poverty line, now this number has increased to 46.2 million. If in 2008, 30 million people were on food stamps, now 46.6 million citizens receive food stamps. The unemployment rates among Hispanic and black people are the highest ever. The systematic extension of unemployment benefits made people reluctant to search for and get real jobs. Democrats insisted and Republicans agreed to these extensions. Because of this excessive support, people were discouraged from retraining and searching for jobs actively.

However, the more people became poor, the more the Democrats gained voter base. President Obama contributed to these sad statistics because he thought that creating government jobs would reduce unemployment and poverty levels. In fact, government cannot create jobs; it creates favorable conditions for private businesses to create jobs. Obamacare, wrong energy policies, and financial regulation have blocked the economy's blood vessels – banks and financial institutions - from making decisions for themselves and their customers. Businesses are paralyzed by these circumstances. All these policies contributed to the increased poverty.

Chapter 8
Wars

President Obama takes credit for killing the number one terrorist. However, the intelligence about Bin Laden's courier was obtained during Bush's presidency. Additionally, intelligence agencies and Navy Seals did this job. Obama's task was to agree or disagree to take down Bin Laden. Obama ended the Iraq War, which indeed was unnecessary. The country spent over $500 billion on it and over four thousand brave man and women paid the ultimate price with their lives. In exchange, Iraq has taken no obligation to reimburse that tremendous spending. It is not even loyal to the USA anymore. It helps Iran access Syria through its territory that provides weapons and other support to help Syria's Assad to kill his own citizens. Wars are always bad.

To maintain national security, the war on terror is justified. However, nation building in hopes that people get educated and take our side is illusion. Religious beliefs in Afghanistan are superior to any other things. As far as the Taliban remain untouched and uninvolved in the reconciliation process, they will remain the same over many decades if U.S. occupation lasts that long. They always will impose their medieval culture. There is no reason for NATO forces being in Afghanistan if they cannot wipe out the Taliban (kill every single one) or reconcile the nation. NATO has to do one of them. Otherwise, as soon as NATO exits Afghanistan in 2014, the Taliban will take over and the country will be a safe haven for Al-Qaida again. Afghan government is corrupt (has no superior values. The Taliban's superior values are religion) and it will not be able to hold up.

All these years were wasted assuming that NATO should not negotiate with terrorists. The Taliban actually did not participate in terrorist acts on U.S. soil. Al-Qaida did. All Taliban, but Mulla Omar (a relative of Bin Laden) and some extremist wings, should be involved in the peace process. It could be reasonable that the Taliban change their organization's name to a civilized political party name. Without achieving a political solution to the problem, withdrawing troops from Afghanistan will not be classified as victory. Sometime, it will be necessary to go to a new war in the same place for the same reason.

Ayman al-Zawahiri is still alive. He has been more active than Osama Bin Laden over the last few years with recorded tapes, videos, and Internet messages signaling terrorists their next plans. He is active today. The attack on the U.S. Consulate in Benghazi, Libya, should be assumed to have been perpetrated by him. A Republican president might handle the Afghan issue differently than President Obama, who wasted time trying to keep imaginary peace in Afghanistan. Almost nothing has been done. Training police forces and army will not yield any positive results if the nation is polarized. More and more NATO troops are being killed by trainees. Russians used the same methods which did not work.

Chapter 9
Avoidance

President Obama actually did not work full-time in the White House. He had very rare cabinet meetings as if there were no significant issues to discuss and make consensus decisions. Obama did not work with the Congress as he should have. When Democrats controlled both Chambers of Congress, he worked with Democrats only. When Democrats lost the House in 2010, he stopped working with both Chambers. The U.S. has the most powerful legislative institution in the world and it decides most world problems. It was abandoned by the U.S. President. The President has to work with Congress and not vice versa. President Reagan worked hard every day with the Congress and was happy to relax a bit because sometimes Congress recessed. President Clinton worked with Congress closely and listened to it in making decisions. He helped create over 20 million jobs and the economy was growing and the country thriving. In those conditions, Clinton understood that national health care overhaul would damage not only the country but also his chances to get reelected. Speaker of the House in Clinton times, Newt Gingrich, deserves a great appreciation from President Clinton and American people.

The President's main concern was to escape the workplace. He played over 100 rounds of golf in three and half years while the country was in big trouble. He had over 200 domestic trips in three and half years and had hundreds of town hall meetings in states. They mainly were about his agenda and preparation for the next presidential elections. Forty-two percent of his trips were in a few swing states. Those meetings mainly were a type of campaign fund raising event. To my mind, the main reason for escaping the workplace was the lack of understanding of the whole scope of duties of the President of the United States. Obama took the office to entertain himself. On many occasions he met celebrities in the White House. Some celebrities visited him several times. He assumed that the presidency would be full of fun. Obama sent Air Force One to picture New York's skyline, flying very low and scaring thousands of tourists and people of the major U.S. city which suffered from the terrorist attacks of Islamist extremists flying low to hit the twin towers of the World Trade Center. That was one of his self-entertaining events. Nobody knows if he was on board or not. Sometime Americans will know what indeed happened on that day.

It seems to me that American youth who voted for him handed over to Obama a big toy which is called the United States of America and Air Force One, and he plays with them as he wants. He has fully ignored Congress over the past two years (2011-2012). He undermined the Supreme Court, calling it an unelected body. Instead of focusing on neutralizing the consequences of economic recession, he dealt with Obamacare over one and half years and did nothing to help the country recover from economic recession. Instead, he worsened the situation with excessive regulations.

Foreign trips were part of his personal entertainment. They did not bring anything beneficial. Instead, he reached an agreement with Russia to reduce drastically the U.S.'s nuclear warheads that serve as a shield to protect the country from enemies. He thinks that the U.S. does not have enemies. Did he read minds of such people as Putin, Chavez, Ahmadinejad, Kim, and others?

The agreement with Russia to reduce nuclear warheads to 1500 from over 5000 in one shot breaches the country's national security. Other trips also were fruitless. Especially his China trip brought nothing positive in establishing fair trade. China continues manipulating its currency. The membership in the World Trade Organization assumes that the member countries do not manipulate their currencies and trade practices.

President Obama did not have a meeting with his national security team to take security measures for the anniversary of 9/11. This day always was dangerous. After the Arab spring, in many countries power shifted from dictators to some type of democracies and they do not or are not able to control violent behavior in the streets. He did not have a National Security Council meeting on the day when the U.S. diplomats were killed in Libya. Instead, Obama kept campaigning on that day in Las Vegas. He is not a type of leader who can see all the little details and nuances of leadership roles. Generating donations and distributing funds among disadvantaged people does not require much leadership as Obama did when he was a community organizer. The Ambassador's and three other Americans' death might have been prevented if President Obama had stayed in his office and made appropriate decisions.

He did not do much in his office in terms of both domestic and foreign policy. Therefore, the economy is struggling, the country is losing in the trade war, the Middle East burning, Iran is close to obtaining nuclear weapons, Russia is helping out our enemies (Obama naively thinks that we do not have enemies), China is overtaking the U.S. economy in trade. Instead of meeting foreign leaders in the General Assembly of the United Nations in New York, he went to a series of reality and late night TV shows, meeting with celebrities to expose himself to voters. The President has done nothing to accelerate recovery after the recession and has contributed much to the stagnation of the U.S. and world economy.

Chapter 10
Negligence

President Obama as the head of the executive branch of government has to enforce existing laws and newly adopted laws under his presidency. However, because of his limited leadership experience and capabilities, he failed to enforce the federal immigration laws. States took measures to enforce them on their own, adopting state laws. When they did so, his administration sued states. Arizona law that mandates checking immigration status of people if stopped by local police because of traffic or other violations was overturned by the Supreme Court. Illegal immigrants are free to live and work and commit crimes because immigration laws are not enforced by the federal government as they should be. Something was being done on deportation of people who illegally crossed U.S. borders. However, it slowed down after Obama's executive order not to deport a certain category of illegal immigrants. Deportation is a very expensive activity and a measure against consequences of events rather than causes of events. The causes of illegal immigration are weak border control and inadequate surveillance by the federal government.

Nothing is done to strengthen the fence between the U.S. and Mexico. The existing fence is designed conveniently to climb over. I did not see any smooth clean fence. All parts of it have texture to hold your body firmly on the fence. Other countries have multiple lines of fencing and even powered fences. Knowing that, no one would attempt to cross borders.

President Obama neglects to enforce laws and regulations as prescribed by the Constitution. Instead, he issues executive orders to disable some provisions of the federal laws. Another example is the executive order to allow some states not to enforce work requirements in the welfare law. The law requires that to be eligible for welfare, citizens have to actively search for employment. Now, people are eligible for welfare without any obligations. This dramatically increases federal spending on welfare programs. It is not a secret that many businesses have openings for low-paying jobs, but people are not going to take them.

The President made several appointments in his cabinet without the Senate's confirmation when the Senate was in recess. He often neglects regular daily in-person briefings on national security and requires written information. It is unknown if he reads or does not read these documents. Based on the security breach in the Benghazi consulate, he did not read information about possible 9/11 anniversary threats. He neglected his responsibility to hold a National Security Council meeting to discuss the Benghazi situation.

Chapter 11
Dissension

President Obama's ideology and ideas are inconsistent with the values of this country and therefore he was not able to work with Republicans or even with his own Democrats and was not able to reach compromise on the fundamental issues that affect the lives of Americans. The Congress encountered strong pressure to promote Obama's agenda that its members could not recognize and sometimes got lost because the programs could not be funded.

First, Obamacare was adopted strictly on party lines by Democrats in the House and Senate. No one Republican voted for it because this pact would overtake one sixth of the economy. Many countries have public health care systems. However, quality of health care because of nationalization dramatically is dramatically lower. Most research is conducted and breakthroughs are made in private medicine where there is high motivation and sufficient funding to do so. Over the last twenty years, sixty three percent (29/46) of Nobel- prize winners in physiology and medicine were Americans. Socialized medicine imposes strong governmental control and some essential areas of research will be abandoned because of rationing, shortage of funding, and low demand.

Second, President Obama was not able to compromise with Republicans on the stimulus bill too. Democrats adopted that bill and over $500 billion dollars were distributed among states and preferred businesses. This money allowed states to maintain their spending. They might cut their spending in hard times and nothing would happen if they tightened belts for a while until the recession would pass. States using the federal stimulus money continued spending as they did before. Of course, some insignificant appropriation cuts occurred in states.

Third, President Obama's budget proposals have never been approved by both chambers of Congress: The House of Representatives and Senate. Amazingly, no one Democrat voted for three annual budget proposals that Obama's administration made. Therefore, Obama completely ignored Congress over the past two years. Obama's ideology and practices do not fit the American way of life.

Encountering opposition in Congress, Obama started issuing executive orders that breached existing laws adopted by Congress. Specifically, the immigration law prescribes deportation of illegal immigrants. Obama waived this provision of the immigration law for certain categories of illegal immigrants. The welfare law requires recipients to retrain and actively search for a job. Obama waived this provision of the law, allowing recipients not to retrain and seek a job. So, an unemployed person may be eligible for welfare over an undetermined time or always.

Obama's dissension led to $5.4 trillion new federal in debt that the future generations have to pay off. If he compromised, Congress might find the best ways to control the debt. To reduce debt, Obama wants to increase taxes in the new recession even though he stated that it would be a bad decision to increase taxes at such times. His plan increases taxes to individuals and businesses whose income is over $250 thousand. Note that all the small businesses make over this amount. Therefore, increased taxation involves all the small businesses that usually create most jobs. The
Congress was able to prevent Obama from implementing this idea so far. But he insists that he would increase taxes while other countries, including Japan (which has the highest tax rates), are decreasing tax rates to let businesses have some funding to create new jobs. As Bush's tax cuts expire, tax rates

automatically increase for everybody on January 1 of 2013.

Chapter 12
Foreign Policy

President Obama tried to be nice to everybody and lost the ability to distinguish enemies from friends. He decided that every country was America's friend. Enemies cannot turn into friends overnight. His speech in Cairo changed the world to the worse so far. The Arab spring denounced friends-dictators. They were forced to resign or killed or exiled by unknown opposition forces which may or may not be friends of America. Some of the opposition may be affiliated with Al-Qaida and other terrorist organizations. Al-Qaida originated from Egypt's Muslim Brotherhood. Elections were held and citizens of Egypt elected their president who is the head of Muslim Brotherhood. Egypt may be another Iran. Germany's Hitler, Italy's Mussolini, and Japan's Hideki Tōjō were elected democratically and later turned into fascists. Japanese Prime Minister Tōjō was responsible for the Pearl Harbor attacks and was in alliance with Hitler. Fundamentalist Islam is inconsistent with democracy because it insists on enforcing Sharia law which is extremely oppressive. It is politicized and promotes oppressive political systems run by religious or non-religious political figures. Fundamentalists rule Iran and Egypt. Dictators rule most Muslim countries. Libya and Tunisia are emerging countries with an unclear political future. Pakistani, Indonesian, and Malaysian democracies are shaky.

Provoking youth in Egypt, President Obama fueled the most dangerous parts of the Muslim world. The most active citizens in those countries are associated with local religious extremist organizations. The President was supposed to anticipate these events and was not supposed to promote democratic ideas in this region. Democracy can be established if at least part of the society is ready for it as in India. In Muslim countries societies do not have civilized opposing forces. The most active part of those societies is organized fundamentalist Islam. Democratically elected Egyptian President Morsi will be the next Egyptian dictator. The latest developments with anti-American protests and killings of American diplomats are a direct result of President Obama's amateur foreign policy. You cannot approach problems of this volatile region irresponsibly. Local religious groups associated with Al-Qaida are taking over countries after revolutions supported by the West. The irony is that the West supports Islamists associated with AL- Qaida to take down secular dictators. And then it boomerangs the West with this kind of protest and killings that happened in Benghazi.

The Libyan government did not have any security measures that could protect the U.S. consulate. It is unknown if the attack was a joint operation of the Libyan government, Islamists, former supporters of Kaddafi, and Al-Qaida. Syria's revolution may produce similar outcomes. The Muslim World's most brutal dictatorships are associated with Russia. It is possible that Egypt will be under Russia's umbrella soon. The immediate outcome is that the national security and interests of the United States are in jeopardy in the Muslim World.

PART III

PRESIDENT OBAMA'S CHEAP SHOTS

Because President Obama's economic policies did not work, unemployment rates remain high, gas prices are skyrocketing, food prices doubled, spending and federal debt are out of control, foreign policy is failing. He is making cheap shots to divide the nation and provide some incentives to specific groups of voters so that they will reelect him. He suggests to pool together with him, with the government. Individuals that are able to work have to be responsible to provide for their own lives and the government has to provide security as it is stated in the Constitution. Government cannot provide food and welfare to those who have no need of those if they have jobs.

Government has to perform its own duties: defend and maintain national security which is under scrutiny around the world and create a favorable economic and legal environment whereby businesses flourish and create millions of good jobs. The President now is campaigning and offering more and more help to Americans as the communist leaders did in the Soviet Union. This help is not about creating good economic conditions, but giving something tangible to everyone from federal funds for free. On TV, one lady said that she would reelect Obama because he gave her a cell phone. It is amazing to look at his cheap shots.

Chapter 1
Student loans and tax credits

Obama visits college campuses and scares you, young people by saying that interest rates on student loans would double if he does not rescue you from Congress's intentions to do so. Did you realize that Congress has hundreds of smart people representing you and your parents? This scare tactic is to convince you that he is your man, and he will help you and nobody else. Do you understand the whole scope of the President's responsibilities? Do you understand what he has done to the country? His destructive policies stopped businesses functioning normally. He denounced the traditional energy sources (oil and coal) and focused on green energies that do not cover even ten percent of the country's needs. His policies prevent businesses from expansion and job creation. Do you realize that after graduation from college, you may not be able to find a good job in your major because companies are not hiring?

They are waiting for good days, hoping that those days will come after Obama's presidency. If you are planning to rehire Obama, you are destroying your own future. How excited are your looks when Obama is on your campus! Think a bit and analyze what you could do without any experience at the position of CEO at a large company. You do not know what CEOs do. The same thing happened to Obama. He did not know what presidents do. He was not a governor of a state or even a mayor of a city. He was a community organizer and state senator only.

How can you trust a person who has been training on the job and has not learned anything from that training? Obama did not even try to train on the job because he knew that he was in the wrong place. He just escaped by playing golf, visiting states to conduct campaign type meetings criticizing Congress and republicans. He did not work with the Congress and blamed it as destructive. The President's obligation is to work with Congress no matter how partisan it is. He did not have cabinet meetings over six and more months. He does not know what to discuss in those meetings.

Nobody threatened to increase interest on student loans except him. This narrative is made up. President Obama's scare tactics are cheap shots to get young men and women's votes once again. Many young people who have graduated from college and work in various industries and who voted for Obama now realize that they did a bad mistake. Then they did not understand what would be the outcome of Obama's presidency. They did not care about his experience. They listened to him. Speaking does not mean doing if you do not have competence and capabilities. You can speak about anything, but you cannot do anything if you do not have experience. Obama's speaking all was theory and empty promises. Definitely, those young people will not get fooled twice. However, you may get fooled the first time if you are voting the first time.

Remember, Obama has not changed. He has not learned on the job. He does not understand the poor results of his current policies and even is not trying to do so. He was busy campaigning all these four years. He does not have any vision for the next four years grounded on the country's resource capabilities. His vision is utopian and ungrounded especially as it concerns green energy. He does not know how to make the country competitive again, how to win competition with China and other fast growing economies. He does not know how to handle the Muslim world.

The American Educational Access credit and other tax credits are good support for students and their parents. However, they were done to gain voter loyalty at the expense of the collapsing economy. If the economy collapses, there will be nothing. Everything will be wiped out: jobs, earnings, wealth, homes...

Chapter 2
Contraceptives

President Obama with an executive order mandates insurance companies and consequently organizations, including churches, to provide free contraceptives to their employees. Ironically, he does so at the expense of other insurance holders because insurance companies will not comply at their own expense. They simply raise insurance premiums.

Therefore, it is evident that Obama has made a cheap shot. He thinks insurance companies would do a favor for him and provide additional services for free to clients. They better understand the economics of their businesses. Republicans and the Catholic Church oppose this ridiculous policy.

Democrats denounce this approach of the Republicans and church as war against woman. The goal is to earn not only women's but also men's votes as well, bribing them at the expense of other insurance policy holders. Single women mainly vote democrat despite that no republican president cut their benefits and never removed their safety net. Democrats communicate their message directly, promising what they would provide, while Republicans communicate their message through their economic policies so that citizens provide for themselves. Overall economic growth helps increase the wealth of every single citizen. Democrats are pro-choice and are for women's right to choose to get rid of their unborn child. Republicans are against unnecessary abortion and value life that starts at conception. Many women prioritize their living standards that depend on a healthy economy first and contraceptives and abortion last. Being pro-life does not mean one is at war against women.

Chapter 3
Gay marriage

Another of President Obama's cheap shots is his approval of same sex marriage. This contradicts the Defensive Marriage Act and is not supported by conservatives and the Christian Churches in all white, black, and Hispanic communities. The official definition of marriage is two individuals, one man and one woman, who create a family and produce children to insure the continuity of human life. Being against gay marriage in the past, Obama altered his position on this issue for political reasons to attract and energize the gay community to get their votes. Gay couples might create civil unions and nobody would oppose such unions. However, letting gays marry is offensive to traditionally married people.

Chapter 4
Don't ask, don't tell

The military is the place where people serve the nation and their private life is left behind. It is very distracting to see gay people who openly expose themselves in public places. If it is done in the military, the distraction doubles and triples. Many straight people get angry. Overall, the situation in the military gets tense. Therefore, there was an effective law named "Do Not Ask, Do Not Tell" to make sure that the military is not the place for personal relationships and gay behavior. For Obama, who barely understands what military discipline is, repealing this law was important because he might energize gay troops to vote for him while the military overwhelmingly votes Republican. This is another cheap shot.

Chapter 5
You did not build it

To justify his plans to increase taxes, President Obama suggested that no business was built by their owners, somebody else made it happen. Why then do such things not happen to everybody? Why can't everybody build a business? Everybody is entitled to use roads and bridges, but not everybody can build a business. It takes tremendous effort (hard work) and energy as well as resources to build a business. Obam's narrative is that to the extent that somebody helped build your business, you have to pay higher taxes. No one objects to paying higher taxes if they earn extraordinary profits. Those profits have evaporated because of high energy costs and shrinking opportunities because of wrong economic policies. Businesses will be able to pay more taxes when they expand. Businesses can expand if they pay lower taxes now. New businesses can emerge if the government recognizes that people build businesses, not the government. The Obama administration does not understand this simple arithmetic. Obama lost all the highly qualified economic advisors, including from Harvard University and the University of Chicago. The current chairman of the White House's Council of Economic Advisors has no extended experience in macroeconomics.

Chapter 6
Illegal immigration

President Obama's next cheap shot was postponing deportation of certain categories of illegal immigrants for two years, hoping that their relatives that have voting rights would vote for him. If he was worrying about immigration issues, he would have adopted a comprehensive law on it when Democrats controlled both chambers of the U.S. Congress during the first two years of his presidency. He was not interested in it. In the last minutes, he remembered Hispanic voters and issued an executive order which contradicts the U.S. Constitution. He was not authorized to issue such an order when Congress was in session. Those people that were waived from deportation for two years are eligible to obtain driver's licenses that they may use inappropriately, including for voter registration and voting. If the system of verification of citizenship fails, those people will definitely contribute to Obama's reelection.

Chapter 7
National security leaks

The next cheap shot was leaking extremely important national security information to the press to show how the Obama administration accomplishes certain successes in foreign affairs. The Administration disclosed the name of the Pakistani doctor who helped to locate Osama Bin Laden. Because of this that man was imprisoned for 33 years. The disclosure of information about the Navy Seals that took down Ben Laden, led to the killing of most of those Navy Seals in Afghanistan. Another leak was on cyber-attacks against Iranian computer systems used in its nuclear facilities. There were other leaks of classified information from the State Department and Pentagon that was on the Web site of WikiLeaks.

Chapter 8
Withdrawal from Iraq

The withdrawal of U.S. troops from Iraq was done purely for the purposes of gaining voter loyalty. No residual forces were left behind. No economic or political loyalty was offered by Iraqis. Now Iraq is the main corridor for Iran to transport its weapons to Syria to support Assad's bloody regime which has already killed over 30 thousand of its own citizens. Iraq now is the ally of Iran, the main adversary of Israel and the United States. How ironic is this! War was not ended with victory. It ended with loss with the ultimate sacrifice of the lives of thousands of brave men and women. Tens of thousands of troops wounded. War was meaningless. However, as far as it was fought, it was supposed to end with a victory. Obama was interested in ending it to gain political points only. The country lost political and economic advantage by giving up Iraq to Iran, the worst enemy of modern civilization with its medieval political regime that supports such prominent terrorist organizations as Hesbollah and Hamas.

Chapter 9
Taxing the rich and payroll tax reduction

Obama's intentions to increase taxes for the rich are not in line with other countries' efforts to reduce taxes. Other countries, including Japan, are decreasing taxes in order to let retained profits be used for business expansion and job creation. Capital will flee the U.S. if taxes are raised. No significant tax revenues will be collected. The French government raised tax rates for the rich and many wealthy people are taking or planning to take foreign citizenship. We have some such cases in the U.S. Rich people are fleeing the country. One of them is Facebook's top manager. This is Obama's cheap shot to put the rich against the poor or low income people; to emphasize that there are rich people who became rich at your expense as communists always said. This is Obama's class warfare rhetoric, about which Marx wrote in his *Communist Manifesto*. The Occupy Wall Street movement is the extension of this cheap shot.

The payroll tax reduction was a good decision but the nation could not afford it in the middle of a weak recovery, and it cannot afford it in the middle of a looming double dip recession and skyrocketing national debt. It was a cheap shot to please voters with a little money. The country might afford it if Obama reduced his Solyndra-type spending. Solyndra was granted a loan guarantee from the Department of Energy for over $500 billion and went bankrupt. Some other solar energy plants are also may file for bankruptcy soon.

Chapter 10
Occupy Wall Street

The Occupy Wall Street movement's main demand is income equality and fair taxation. They share President Obama's philosophy. Therefore, he was sympathetic with the movement. Some people assume that the whole idea of occupy belongs to Obama. The Occupy Wall Street movement mainly carries Obama's ideas about income redistribution and taxing the rich. Actually, the well-known corrupt Acorn community organizing group that helped Obama get elected in 2008, with a changed name, was one of the organizers of the Occupy protests. Other top Democrats supported this movement because it advances Obama's agenda on income equality, income redistribution, and higher taxes for the rich.

In socialism, some people work hard and create wealth and others do not do so and get more money. The government stands in the middle and redistributes that wealth. This type of formula is going to be used in the USA. By nature people are different (unequal) in their abilities, skills, and knowledge, as well as effort. Therefore, people earn different amounts of income. There is nothing wrong with this state of affairs. Market determines the price of labor. If your skills and abilities are exceptional, you will be hired for high-paid jobs. Your income will be unequal to the income of those people who have fewer skills and abilities. Why do the high earners have to share their income with those who did not put more effort into developing their skills and abilities? The disabled and elderly are excluded because they are eligible for benefits.

Obama's ideology is to provide for those people who can work but do not want to work as in Venezuela or Cuba. If income is redistributed and income equality is achieved, there will be no incentives to work better, put forth more effort, and make more money than others as in the Soviet Union, a former communist country that collapsed because of this very factor.

Taxation is good and everybody is willing to pay taxes. But tax money must be spent to address the government's constitutional duties: national security, defense, and support of those citizens who are not able to support themselves. Obama is going to support those who are able to support themselves, expanding Medicaid within Obmacare. That is expensive and the mandate has already stopped business from growing.

Excessive taxing of the rich will push capital out of the country. They will invest their capital somewhere else. If necessary, they will change their citizenship. It always happened, but may be very intense if Obama lets taxes go up. Anticipating tax hikes, U.S. billionaires and millionaires are waiting Obama's and Congress's decision on this sensitive issue and are holding their capital instead of investing in the U.S. economy. Initiating and supporting the Occupy movement to promote his agenda on these matters is a cheap shot. If the economy had been put on the right track from the beginning of Obama's presidency, these cheap shouts would not be necessary. Everybody would be happy to reelect him. Who wants their President to fail? The failure of the President means the failure of the country and the failure of every citizen.

Chapter 11
Tetchy

President Obama stated that he won the election and therefore Congress would do whatever he wants. That was a cheap shot. He dismissed more than 47% of voters who did not vote for him. He dismissed the fact that the Congress was elected by Americans too and had members representing the opposition Republican Party. Confrontation started from there. He was sensitive to every criticism that the other party expressed. In order not to hear criticism, Obama ordered crafting of Obamacare behind closed doors.

Republicans were not the authors of Obamacare and obviously did not have their own version. However, they had serious concerns about its key provisions such as the mandate and expanded Medicaid and its cost to the federal and state budgets. Obama's main problem was his inability to take criticism and work together with Congress to reach compromises. Campaigning in swing states, he calls for working together with voters while he did not work with members of Congress whom voters sent to Washington to work on their behalf. President Clinton worked across the aisle and reached compromises on every issue. By contrast, President Obama rejected any compromise. The reason for that was that he had to keep his numerous utopian promises made in the presidential campaign of 2008. The wasted stimulus package was adopted to fulfill those promises. He chose to use his power to issue executive orders during Congressional recesses or other times, abusing power. Obama prized news networks that did not notice his mistakes in domestic and foreign policy and condemned media that criticized his wrong policies.

Chapter 12
Unemployment benefits

President Obama's administration prevented businesses from being successful and creating new jobs with the imposed Dodd-Frank Act and Obamacare and energy policies. Because of huge numbers of unemployed people, Obama extended unemployment benefits up to two years. Republicans voted for several extensions with Democrats instead of coming up with long term solutions. Democratic Senate never tried to think strategically. Additionally, the government issued an executive order to waive work requirements for welfare benefits. Now unemployed people do not have to retrain and actively search for a job to obtain such benefits in several states. There are many job openings in the service and manufacturing and those low-paying jobs are not filled. That was a new cheap shot to gain voter loyalty from unemployed citizens.

Chapter 13
Obamacare waivers

It was evident that business would struggle to implement Obamacare which mandates all businesses
to provide health insurance to all their employees: full-time and part-time. Therefore, some powerful members, of Congress such as Nancy Polosi granted

them wavers from Obamacare in their districts. This was a cheap shot of the Obama administration choosing good and bad people and businesses and favoring some over others. Starting in 2014, most Americans will be charged a penalty if they fail to buy insurance.

The Internal Revenue Service (IRS), which collects taxes, indicated recently that its agents will not be involved in tax audits, to pursue Americans without health insurance. What does this mean? Does not Obamacare charge IRS to do so? To my mind, it does because the IRS has thousands of staff to overview Obamacare and it must be implemented as far as the Supreme Court upheld it. Is it not another cheap shot? It misleads people because if an audit is not done, penalties will not be charged. If the IRS does not audit taxpayers, people may not buy health insurance. How will Obmacare be funded then? The IRS is misleading and wants to say that there is nothing bad is coming along, so vote for Obama. It may happen that Obamacare may not be implemented even if Obama is reelected. Obama is interested in the process rather than implementation. He can think but never worry about implementing right policies.

He has already breached existing laws. Why not to breach his own laws?

Chapter 14
"Middle class" slogan

President Obama, Vice President Biden, and their campaign use multiple times in short statements the words "middle class" that they basically do not care about. Their policies increased the number of poor people and shrank the middle class by at least seven million people. Recessions end quickly or slowly depending on policies put forth by the federal government, specifically the executive branch, the head of which is President Obama. Recovery from the recession was lengthy and very weak because of Obama's bad economic policies proposed by him and approved by the Democrats in Congress strictly on party lines. In 2011, the number of poor increased to 15.7% from 13% in 2008 and 15.1% in 2010.

Obama's poor economic policies are responsible for all this. Those policies are war against traditional energy sources oil, coal, and nuclear power; the brutal financial regulation that prevents banks from lending to businesses; and Obamacare that imposes a cost-inefficient burden on businesses. Now Obama is promising something else unknown to the middle class. Because of the three factors listed above businesses are not hiring and are reducing their workforce and middle-class families are losing jobs. Bank of America announced that it will cut 16000 middle-class jobs soon this year.

Obama's failed foreign trade and investment policies resulted in losing more manufacturing jobs to foreign countries. In these conditions, how can Obama promise something to the middle class? Obama will continue this policy further in his second term if reelected. The poverty levels will increase because there is only one way to get out of it: job creation. Obama's way is to support more and more people that cannot support themselves because of they cannot find jobs. Would this lead to prosperity? Obama always talks about a fair shot. However, Obama is reducing all the chances to get fair shot to millions. According to Obama, fair shot is obtaining support (welfare benefits) from the government through redistribution. Obama does not recognize that good jobs strengthen the middle class and reduces poverty.

The Republican-controlled House introduced and adopted a jobs bill. However, the democrat controlled Senate will not vote on it. The House adopted a coal energy bill, the Senate will not vote on it. If adopted, Obama promised to veto it. Why? Because it will be a Republican bill: nothing Republican can go through the Senate and the President because it will undermine Obama's accomplishments and reduce his chances of being reelected. Young people have to understand how dangerous it is to keep Obama in office four more years.

Obama also is planning to tax families who make over $250 thousand a year. These households belong to the upper middle class. Almost all small business families make around or over $250 thousand and Obama's plan increases taxes to most small businesses. You may say, I am not making that amount of money and I do not care about them paying more taxes. If they pay more taxes, they will lay you off because they will not be able to afford you to work for them. Your friend, siblings, or parents may lose their jobs too. That is why Obama's tax plan is dangerous to the middle class and anyone else. The term "middle class" that Obama is using is scam.

He is not for but against the middle class.
This is another of his cheap shots.

Chapter 15
Benghazi situation

The situation in Benghazi was a
terrorist attack and there was no
demonstration at around 10 PM on 9/11 of
2012. Somebody already knew that the
Ambassador was there and signaled to
terrorists and they came along fully
equipped with heavy weapons. The
intelligence sources confirmed within 24
hours that it was an organized terrorist
attack. The Consulate staff was in direct
phone contact with the administration when
the terrorist attack was under way and
provided real-time information which
should have confirmed that it was a
terrorist attack. The Obama administration
knew that it was a terrorist attack way
ahead of the media appearance of the U.S.
Ambassador to the U.N. The Ambassador
announced that it was a demonstration
turned violent against a video that was
posted on YouTube by an American of
Egyptian descent. Additionally, the U.S.
Embassy in Libya multiple times asked for
security enhancement, and all the requests
were denied and even existing security was

mostly withdrawn by the Obama administration.

In fact, the Obama administration did not want people to know that a terrorist attack occurred on Obama's watch. This was a new cheap shot to mislead voters into thinking that Obama was successful against terrorism even if he never used the term terrorism to describe the actions of terrorists. After 9/11 of 2001, no terrorist attack occurred against U.S. interests. On Obama's watch three terrorist attacks occurred on U.S. soil: The Fort Hood shooting, Arkansas shooting, and Benghazi explosions that killed four Americans. Obama dismissed all of them as terrorist attacks and called them workplace violence or just violence.

If Muslims wanted to protest, they might do so in July when the YouTube video went out. They aimed for the day of 9/11 in order to demonstrate that they hate America and its policies in the Middle East. So, Obama's policies in that region were not good enough. Obama wanted to emphasize that Muslims are not against U.S. policies but against the video. All the Muslim countries have extremist groups and political forces and they also make politics in those countries. Their governments quietly support them. Otherwise, they would have cracked down on the embassy attackers severely. Where are the attackers? Where were Libya's security forces? If they were engaged in the five-hour-battle, where were the losses among attackers or Libyan forces?

Chapter 16:
Democratic Party Convention

The Democratic Party's convention mainly was about promising something to everybody if they vote Democrat. That something may be given for free as contraceptives. Marx said that in communism everybody will contribute as much as they can and receive from the society as much as they want. If we change the phrase "as much as they can" to "as much as the government wants from taxpayers," it is mainly about income redistribution. This resembles Obama's fair shot (getting from the government as much as possible) and fair share (paying taxes as much as possible) slogan. A fair shot is about getting from society more and more, not giving a little or nothing back. You do not have to put both much individual effort as Obama did while working as a president but get as much as you want (long-term unemployment benefits and free health care through the expanded Medicaid...). This experiment has been conducted in the Soviet Union and ended with its collapse. This policy kills incentives to work hard, create more, and earn more.

President Obama has not confiscated private property so far (bailouts are actually governmental takeover of the bailed out companies). However, with his policies, private ownership of means of production may become obsolete. Many will be willing to sell their businesses and depart for other places, for example for Singapore, Hong Kong, Taiwan, or Mainland China. Obama's idea about redistribution of wealth will demolish this country because the main engine of capitalism – INCENTIVES –will be gone. The main message of Democrats was that government would take care of people. Even if they do not believe in the effectiveness of this, they have no choice but to say so. They need people's votes.

Obama is desperate to stay in the White House no matter what happens with the country which is gravely sick because of his policies. Why is Europe in economic turmoil? Because it's main customer, the United States of America, is in economic and political turmoil, and demand for European products is very low in the USA. If the economy of the USA grows, Europe's economy grows. Obama's policies hold the entire globe in hostage. Therefore, these elections are crucial.

It is interesting that Obama does not criticize Hugo Chavez, and Chavez is ready to vote for Obama if he were a U.S. citizen. Why? Both of them have a common socialist ideology – redistribution of wealth. Instead of talking about distribution of wealth, he should have been talking about minimum wage increase, production of import-substituting products, expanding manufacturing, achieving fair trade agreements, making China stop its currency manipulation, and so many other things that will help put this country back on the right track. In that case the middle class and America are better off.

Chapter 17
Beer recipe

A new cheap shot is to share the White House's beer recipe with beer drinkers, hoping to get their votes.

Hopefully, beer drinkers would think before voting. They need good jobs too. To buy beer or brew beer you have to have a decent income. You may have a job now, but tomorrow you may not have it because Obama's failed economic policies are causing a new recession.

Chapter 18
Wide and nice smile

You are excited about President Obama's pretty smile. Smile does not deliver product. Smile does not mean anything in terms of leading this country, which has not been led since Obama took office. Obama flashes the same smile in every event multiple times. It is good to watch a nicely smiling president to admire. However, this smiling man's performance is dismal. The greatest country on Earth wasted four years to have the most incompetent president in its history. So much wealth was wasted.

On the day when U.S. Ambassador Christopher Stevens and three more Americans were killed in Benghazi, Obama went to Las Vegas and was all smiles to the crowd. It was such a sad day. It was the day when Obama's Muslim world doctrine was falling apart. Obama failed to secure foreign diplomats from terrorist attacks.

You cannot put food on your kitchen table on Obama's smile. If you vote again loving his smile and charm, you will shut off future opportunities for yourself, siblings, friends, your children and parents. His spending is overwhelming and the national debt will collapse this great country. The country's economy is growing very poorly.

China and others have overtaken manufacturing of this country. Most goods and commodities are imported from China. Now it is seeking expansion of its businesses in the U.S. to gain substantial property. China grows its economy with the help of U.S. companies doing business there, collects taxes from U.S. companies, increases its military power using this money, threatens the U.S. ally Japan, funds one of the worst enemies of the U.S. and its own people North Korea, and finally lends the U.S. money earned from the U.S. companies that outsource their operations to China. These companies do not pay taxes to the U.S. government which is in debt up to its ears. Is it not ironic? Why is the most admired country on Earth giving up everything? Additionally, according to polls, the country is going to reelect an incompetent and weak politician to the highest office who does not understand capitalist economics and foreign policy after four years of tenure as president.

Chapter 19
Character Assassination

Bain Capital

President Obama has made a great effort to assassinate former governor of Massachusetts Romney's character to put him out of the race, distorting his past record which was very positive and successful. Obama does not mention his own record because it is poor. Romney founded Bain Capital – a private equity firm that helped companies to restructure and improve their performance. In some cases companies excited industries because they were going to do something else or close down because of natural competition. The company helped them exit industries with less pain to their employees. This is a normal way that a capitalist economy functions. Every single private enterprise is founded to make profits. If not, there is no reason to waste effort and energy.

The society expects companies to be profitable. Bain Capital was. Obama is blaming Romney that he outsourced jobs overseas. Some companies who received Bain Capital's support might outsource jobs to other countries. This is not illegal. Note that under Obama's policies hundreds of thousands of jobs were outsourced to foreign countries every year. Outbound foreign direct investments exceed inbound investment as much as double. This is simply a cheap shot.

The Obama campaign linked Romney to the death of a woman who died six years after her husband lost his job in one of the companies where Bain Capital provided financial service. She had her own health insurance during the few years after her husband lost his job. That was another cheap shot.

Rich against poor

Obama portrays Romney as a rich guy and out of touch. He says that Romney would not understand the needs of regular folks. If Obama understands people much better than Romney does, why has he let this country decline, leading to another recession? No one of his policies worked

because governmental regulations invented by the Obama administration prevent companies from growing and succeeding.
If private business does not create wealth, where is Obama going to generate tax revenues to redistribute?

Obama believes in income redistribution. Romney believes that every individual is capable of producing income that is sufficient to support the individual if the government creates favorable conditions for success. Romney is going to create an opportunity society where every individual has a fair shot to support him- or herself. Obama is going to create a society where every individual has a fair share shot to get help from the government without putting forth much effort to succeed. This country always succeeded following Romney's philosophy. This is another cheap shot against Romney and to win votes.

Foreign accounts

It is your discretion to keep your wealth anywhere else after paying required taxes. President Obama criticized Romney for having offshore accounts. Think about this. If you are not sure that domestic banks would produce more profits on your investment, why would you not choose a bank which does so anywhere else? Why did Obama not do so? He simply was not a businessman and did not create wealth and is not able to understand how to manage capital effectively and efficiently. If he was, he might do the same thing. It is simply a cheap shot to put Romney against regular folks. Regular folks will be successful if they put forth extra effort be so. Regular folks will be able to find good jobs if business people like Romney are successful.

Foreign policy

Obama says that Romney has no foreign policy experience. Obama did not have any such experience when he became president. Romney governing a state had many occasions to deal with foreign counterparts. The Salt Lake City Olympics were not just a domestic project. Obama's foreign policy did not work in any directions that benefited the United States. The country is a hostage of Chinese product invasion. As Romney says, China manipulates its currency to make local producers competitive globally. He has not done anything to turn Russia around to the path of democracy. It is getting more autocratic and supports brutal dictators from Iran and Syria to Venezuela and Cuba.

Auto industry

Obama and Biden blame Romney because he was against the bailout of the auto industry. Obama thinks that he rescued this industry. This is untrue. Romney said that all the troubled companies were supposed to file Chapter 11 to undergo managed bankruptcy that would save bailout money. Obama chose to bail out first, wasting $20 billion, and then let General Motors and Chrysler undergo bankruptcy protection, wasting precious time. That is another cheap shot.

Romney Tax Returns

President Obama demanded that Romney disclose his tax returns and said that Romney had something to hide. This distrust was groundless because a man who was running for public offices multiple times would not violate any laws that would discredit him. This was a cheap shot too to portray Romney as a law breaker. Some Obama advisers asserted that

Romney might have committed a felony with his tax returns. Obama's main goal was to portray Romney as an ineligible person to be president. Looking at Obama's record, what would you say? This is a big question. There is a great chance not to make another mistake that would work against you and your parents, friends, the society at large. This society should not be transformed into a socialist society like Venezuela.

PART IV
WAKING UP AND SAVING AMERICA

Chapter 1
Growing economy and foreign trade

The country's economic conditions are measured by the growth rates of gross domestic product (GDP). According to official reports, U.S. GDP growth was 2.4% in 2010, it was 1.8 in 2011, and in 2012, the economy slowed down from quarter to quarter. It was 2% in the first quarter, 1.3% in the second quarter. We are in a new prerecession already. When Ronald Reagan took office, the unemployment rate was 9.7% and because of his policies it went down to 7 % in his first term, and the economy grew at 6-7% annually. Over 6 million jobs were created during his first term. The economy has to grow if the government creates favorable conditions and reduces its interference in it.

Deregulation always freed enterprises to succeed. President Obama's financial regulation authored by Senator Dodd and Representative Frank cut off the blood vessels of the U.S. economy. Money is not flowing into it as usual. Borrowing money is much more complicated, especially for small and medium-sized businesses. Large businesses are struggling with competition from China and elsewhere. Cheap imported products are flooding the country and local businesses do not know what to do with their own products and employees. What is needed in this situation is to be clear about the country's national interests. Which is good for the country: letting U.S. companies outsource their businesses and bring back cheap manufactured products from abroad or make those businesses produce their products at home and create wealth for Americans?

Domestic companies that do business overseas do not pay taxes from their foreign profits to the U.S. government nor do they contribute to the society. It is questionable if they bring back any financial resources to inject into the country's economy. It is clear that sales taxes collected from their products originated in foreign countries and sold in the USA help a little. Is it reasonable to protect the country's interests by restricting imports and producing import substituting products in the U.S. as China does? China is a member of the World Trade Organization and nothing is happening to it when it violates its Charter. Or China has to be disciplined? It should be fair if the U.S. concludes a fair trade agreement with

China as soon as possible to reduce imports from China and to help expand domestic manufacturing. Some unique products must be produced domestically and sold at premium prices around the world to make them cost- effective. Especially high-end products should be produced domestically. Of course, some patriotism is demanded from relevant companies.

The government has to have a sense of urgency and decide to optimize foreign trade so that imports must be substituted by domestically produced products. It is true that domestically produced products will be more expensive. However, their quality will be higher. Children might play with two or three toys instead of 20 Chinese manufactured toys. China allows foreign imports to flows into the country with caution, regulates its foreign trade, and manipulates its currency. The artificially set low course of Chinese currency makes Chinese products cheaper than products from anywhere else. Free trade should not be so free if you have national interests and the country's survival at stake and poverty rates are dramatically increasing.

The next president has to define the priorities in foreign trade and the country's manufacturing. I think Europe has to do the same thing in its trade with China. Advanced nations have to support one another if they want to preserve their fundamental principles: capitalism, free enterprise, and the status of being advanced nations. And finally, they should worry about their people first and then people of other countries. The simple thing to do is to reach bilateral trade agreements with all the countries that export their products to the U.S. to balance foreign trade. Only this step will put the U.S. economy on the right track. However, it is not enough. Energy policy must be right.

I think young people in this great country made a serious miscalculation (if they ever made any calculations) electing Obama in 2008. The country has lost an additional trillion dollars in GDP. Average household income has decreased by more than four thousand dollars. People lost 40% of their wealth: real estate values decreased by this percentage. When asked questions relevant to this performance, President Obama was not able to give solid answers in the first presidential debate on October 3 of 2012.

Chapter 2
Increasing energy production

High oil prices contributed to cost inefficiency of transportation, farm production, construction, and all other industries. Price of all goods and food dramatically increased and demand fell significantly because of lowered purchasing power of consumers. Therefore, you see slowed economic growth in the Obama years. Decreased consumer demand makes businesses reduce production output and reduce the number of employees.

The higher the gas prices, the lower economic growth rates, and the more jobs lost. To cut oil prices the world community has to work with OPEC. If possible, such a monopolistic cartel has to be dissolved. Every country has to decide how much oil to produce. Countries have to be motivated to produce more oil. Domestic oil production has to be significantly increased in order to cut oil prices domestically and internationally. The government has to ban oil exports or refined oil exports until global oil prices come down to reasonable levels. Any restrictions on production of traditional energy sources must be lifted immediately. Coal has to be used without any restrictions. The Environmental Protection Agency's task should not be to ban energy production, but to enforce laws that require measures to ensure clean use of those sources in plants and transportation.

Clean environment is very important. However, can we afford it? As Romney said in the presidential debate, Obama has given a tax break to green energy companies for over $90 billion in one year and Obama did not object. Is not this gambling with taxpayer money? The entire economy is thrown under the bus because of these green energy policies. Obama's Change may be this. However, it cannot be initiated and developed in a recession. It cannot be implemented when cost of implementation is 5.5 times more than the traditional coal generated power. Is not it better to implement cleaning systems in the existing power plants and gradually implement wind and solar energies? Obama's Solyndra went bankrupt losing competition to Chinese solar panel producers. Now the General Services Administration (GSA) under Obama is purchasing solar panels from China to install on the roof of a few federal buildings. How ironic it is!

Chapter 3
Reducing national debt

A slowed economy is not producing sufficient revenues to cover increasing governmental spending on various programs. Obama promised to cut the deficit by half, but he doubled it. He generated over $5.4 billion in debt in three and half years while Bush generated a $4 billion debt in eight years fighting two wars. That incredible amount of debt was generated because of Obama's financial regulation (Dodd-Frank Act), green energy policy, stimulus, and Obmacare. How to stop the debt from growing rapidly and how to dissipate it? Obama has no solution to it except taxing the rich. This measure will increase revenues to about $700 billion in ten years, $70 billion annually. Is this a good decision? No, it is not because tax hikes make the rich invest less domestically and more internationally, and companies create fewer jobs. The loss of jobs means the loss of tax revenue. Additionally, the tax hikes will make investors flee the country and invest somewhere else because all other countries are significantly decreasing corporate and individual tax rates.

Obama is not suggesting anything else. He talks about change that takes not just one term, but what would that change be? Based on this debt, no change can be implemented. The country's economy collapses if he makes more change in the same direction. Young voters must understand this earlier than later. A young guy says on TV that he would vote for Obama to let him finish his job. Does he realize what job Obama is going to finish?

The debt can be reduced if the economy grows at tremendously high rates – five-six percent annually. In this economy the federal government will be able to generate more tax revenue and cut spending because poverty rates will significantly decrease. Can Obama do so? The answer is no because he has a theory in his mind which is as wrong as Hugo Chavez's theory of socialism. Does he have experience? No, he has not learned on the job. The first presidential debate has demonstrated it. He campaigned during all his first term to get reelected for the second term. Campaigning is not enough for the incumbent president. The President has to work as president in the first place.

Chapter 4
Promoting free enterprise

Obama does not understand the meaning of free enterprise. He can say that the private sector is doing just fine when it is not. He does not understand the struggle of the private sector for survival. He did not do anything to protect domestic producers from imported goods at least to some degree. Other countries do so. Why not respond to them in the same way? It is right that the main principle of free trade is not to subsidize domestic businesses and industries to promote fair competition. However, all those countries that export products to the U.S. do so, subsidize. If free trade is superior to the country's national interests, why do we have national borders? They should also be removed.

Annually around 60 thousand private businesses go bankrupt. Does Obama know about this fact when saying that the private sector is just doing fine? Free enterprise is no longer free. So many regulations and obligations from the government are imposed on them. Many people cannot open even a lemonade stand because of the bureaucratic restrictions. Private enterprises cannot borrow money from banks without meeting the government's restraining requirements. Government is standing between banks and their clients as a barrier. The same thing is happening in health care: government is standing between doctor and patient.

The concept of free enterprise is that people create their businesses freely and run them freely, meeting minimal requirements imposed by the government. Under Obama, private enterprises have to meet maximum requirements. For example, private medical practitioners have to record everything about patients and report to the government. There is no patient privacy anymore. The government regulates health care heavily. What should be done? First the Dodd-Frank Act must be repealed and replaced. Then Obamacare has to be replaced. Third, any restrictions on traditional sources of energy must be removed so that private enterprise can be competitive using less expensive energy sources. Last, all the bail out and stimulus (thank you money to unionized voters) has to be recovered.

Chapter 5
Increasing employment

Obama is mistaken in assuming that government creates jobs. Private businesses create jobs when they are allowed to operate freely. Obama's assumption that construction of roads and bridges would create millions of jobs is wrong because in the times of President Roosevelt road and bridge construction used manual labor and therefore millions of jobs were created on government contracts. Now it is impossible. Today, using modern technologies, two-three people perform tasks of hundreds of people who were engaged in road and bridge construction in Roosevelt's era. Is not this a childish approach?

Millions of highly experienced people are jobless now who were laid off from banks, financial institutions, and regular service and manufacturing firms. Those private enterprises have to come back and grow if the President's policies are right. They are not coming back. They are not hiring because they have no business that can grow, there are no clients or customers. They continue dismissing people. They are waiting for something and good days. Obama's second term will catastrophically worsen the situation. Therefore, the country needs a president who had his own life experience of solving such types of problems. The country cannot afford inexperienced and unlearned president who is inflexible and never listens to the legitimately existing opposition party's opinion. The Jobs bill adopted by the Republican House of Representatives may be blocked by the Democrat controlled Senate. If approved by the Senate, the President may veto it because it was not designed by Democrats.

Unemployment may be reduced only if economic policies are right. Now they are not. To do so, the economy must be deregulated and all the Obama restrictions must be removed to give private businesses freedom to operate. Some transparency should be present so that companies do not fool their stakeholders: shareholders, customers, suppliers, the government, community, and other partners. To create jobs, foreign trade has to be balanced and manufacturing returned to the country. A new energy policy should encourage production of all the types of energy, traditional and renewable. Ethanol production must be suspended because it consumes a lot of corn and other crops diverted from food production. Overall, a relaxed energy policy will help create over four million jobs according to the rough calculations done by the Romney campaign.

Chapter 6
Reforming taxation

Obama's tax plan is to tax the rich more. He may understand or not that this tax increase will not solve the problem of the massive debt. He knows that accusing the rich of being responsible for poverty; he can gain a very wide voter base. He is engaged in class warfare. In fact, he said that when the economy grows slowly, tax hikes would hurt the economy. Then the growth rate of the economy was over 2%. Now it is 1.3%. He contradicts himself. So, Obama does not have any idea what his real taxation policy would be except increasing taxes for households that make over $250 thousand.

In 2009, the right solution might have been to cut taxes more, let the economy come back on its own without any Dodd-Frank Act, and postpone Obamacare, which has about twenty types of taxes in it, some parts of which are already being paid by companies. We are still in recession as far as oil prices are going up and the economy is slowing down. Taking into account this fact, tax rates must be reduced so that company profits can be used to expand and create more jobs. The rates may be drastically lowered so that not only domestic, but foreign investments flow into the country.

Romney suggests cutting taxes 20% across the board and reducing exemptions and loopholes for upper income earners. The Bowles-Simpson plan suggests that, and Obama did not accept this plan. However, he said that he was not against this plan. To learn more about this plan you always can search the Internet.

Chapter 7
Revamping health care system

In fact, Obamacare is a massive government expansion. It mandates companies provide health care benefits no matter what number of employees they have. Many companies cannot afford that drastic increase in spending and therefore cut jobs and stop hiring. Obamacare is a huge program that expands Medicaid and will cost about $2.7 trillion in 10 years. Nobody asked Obama to expand Medicaid, which is part of a safety net for the poor and those who are not poor. It expands automatically as the number of poor increases. Obama decided that not only the poor must be eligible for Medicaid. In terms of this decision, you can see the signs of socialist approach to reform capitalism. This law must be replaced so that citizens may decide to buy or not to buy insurance. Doctors and patients should make decisions on their health care, not the government.

The replacement law should increase competition among insurance companies and doctors. The out-of-network, preexisting conditions, and out-of-state provisions of the insurance rules statutes of Obamacare must be preserved. Customers should be offered catastrophic insurance plans so that they can afford insurance. Those categories of citizens that are supposedly being added to the expanded Medicaid could buy catastrophic insurance plans, and companies where they work might curry some burden but not all of it. Otherwise, businesses will be inefficient. The new system has to work through insurance companies that offer a variety of plans customized to customer categories. Some of them already have those sorts of plans but do not advertise at all. If states want to have comprehensive health care programs, they should do so on their own as Massachusetts did.

Chapter 8
Reforming education

President Obama talks about education much when the government has no funds to improve the system. He has not done anything about education in his first term. He talked about science and technology in the classroom but these were words only. The country needs to reform the school education fundamentally. The U.S. can win global competition only if it has exceptional scientists and engineers. School education has to focus on science and technology and every school has to merge with science and technology centers, and new centers must be opened. The number of hours allocated for non-science subjects must be decreased. As Romney said, schools can be rated, and based on the ratings; parents may choose them for their children. Elementary schools have a reputation in communities and parents always choose school districts to live. However, high schools in most communities, are single schools and there is no option to choose. However, parents would not mind that their kids travel a few more miles to attend a better school.

Chapter 9
Reducing the role of unions

Originally unions were good to protect rights of employees against businesses that literally exploited the work force. Contemporary laws and regulations provide a safety net and governmental support to those who are in need. Companies buy labor based on experience, skills, abilities, and knowledge, and pay accordingly for the effort put forth. Market supply and demand regulate employee and employer relations. Employers always value good employees. Unions push companies to pay more than the market value of the labor force and make them keep bad workers. Therefore, there is no need for unions if we want to have competitive industries and businesses in this country. As long as they exist, they will continue to blackmail corporations to provide excessive benefits that are significantly more than regular folks earn in similar industries in different states.

Unions of both private and public employees must be dissolved. This will increase competitiveness of businesses, industries, and the country. What union bosses do now is to generate enormous amounts of money from membership fees to assign themselves huge salaries and contribute to the Democratic Party's election campaigns. Often they dictate to their members how to vote in elections. They also lobby convenient legislation in Congress.

Chapter 10
Reducing Dependency

American people traditionally were self-reliant and always provided for themselves through hard work, opportunities, and creativity. They preferred independence. However, the government instead of addressing its authorized duties by the Constitution entered the welfare industry and made people dependent on it. Private entities could perform those functions various private pension funds do. Social Security, Medicare, and Medicaid became the most expensive and monstrous programs of all times of the federal government. Part of these programs might address states.

Another governmental welfare business involves unemployment benefits. Why did all these issues become the main task of the federal government? The answer is that to get reelected for the next term, presidential incumbents initiated welfare reforms. Those reforms were conducted to buy votes in upcoming elections. President Obama did the same thing with his Obamacare. He knew that the health care system of the United States was the best in the world and it did not need such governmental intervention. Some cosmetic measures could make it even more efficient and affordable. He chose the worst scenario to expand Medicaid within Obamcare.

Moreover, the law mandates uninsured people purchase health insurance to generate funds to fund the expanded Medicaid. So, thankful citizens would vote for Obama for Obamacare; how simple that is. The expansion of Medicaid is absolutely unnecessary. Catastrophic insurance plans are sufficient for low income families. The safety net includes Medicaid and eligible citizens are protected. The more people are dependent on the government as in the Soviet Union, the more the country will decline as it is happening now.

Chapter 11
Fundamental transformation and
opportunities

The free market is the best place for free people to seek opportunities through hard work and creativity. You never see those kids who worked hard at school and college suffering from uncertainty. All of them are on the job and live their lives as they want. Those kids who were lazy and did not put forth more effort to learn not only at school or college but independently are low income people. Training and retraining add skills that are required on the job. Many are reluctant to do so.

By the Constitution, this country offers unlimited opportunities to succeed. However, the Obama administration's restrictive policies and regulations cut off many free market features of this country. Green energy projects are outside the free market concept. The Obama administration funds them from taxpayer money. General Electric does not pay taxes because it develops green energies. All this is wrong. Hedge funds cannot conduct their operations as usual because of Obama's financial regulations.

The free market economy is about deregulation. If some companies fail because of their wrong doings, the government does not have to jump ahead and regulate strictly all other companies. Enron acted unethically, and the Sarbanes-Oxley Act mandated all companies be transparent. In a free market economy, transparency means the loss of corporate secrets that make them competitive. Not all the companies act unethically. Americans are decent people and the government should not put them on the same page with dishonest people. Some regulations should exist.

The financial crisis prompted the government to adopt the Dodd-Frank Act that limits the free market economy not only in the banking industry, but also in all other industries. You cannot borrow money from banks without meeting the government's increased requirements. Always crises happen and then the economy comes back. Certain measures from the government are obviously required, but not measures that paralyze the economy for good as Obama has done. The new president's task would be to repeal all three acts: Sarbanes Oxley, Dodd-Frank, and Obamacare and replace them with plausible legislation.

Chapter 12
National security and foreign policy

Obama's vision of foreign policy is to make the world a nice place so that countries highly respect one another, and no one country is a bad country and the U.S. must treat them equally. Overall, Obama is a nice guy for everybody or he wants to look like one. Therefore, he is succeeding in his likability assessment. However, the world is diverse. Countries have significantly differing economic, social, and political systems.

Muslim countries have one of the two worst things: secular dictatorships or theocratic regimes. All the revolutions that occurred in Arabic countries in recent years may lead to the theocratic type of governments because they are willing to adopt religious laws instead of constitutions. It is evident that theocratic regimes are not friendly with the Western world. They plan to spread Islam around the world. Those regimes support terrorist organizations that try to gain political power in any single Muslim country. Only secular dictatorship countries may have some sort of constitution and military power that can prevent Islamists from gaining political power.

The relations of the United States with the Muslim world were always strongly measured and carefully conducted. The Obama administration abandoned that approach, assuming that Arab countries can build democracies. Now Egypt is in the hands of the Muslim Brotherhood raised to power through democratic elections which may be the first and last democratic elections because the Muslim Brotherhood will not let other elections be held. Democratically elected Hitler, Mussolini, and Tōjō turned into fascists and initiated World War II. They were removed from power by the fighting of this war. Assuming such a war is not going to happen, Egypt will be under Russia's influence soon, as Iran, North Korea, and Venezuela are.

The world is more complex than Obama assumes. There are friends and adversaries. If you do not distinguish them clearly, you get confused and cannot set up priorities and do not make any progress in promoting U.S. interests which should be the President's number one task in foreign policy. Obama did not view this as such. Foreign policy has to promote U.S. interests using civilized approaches through negotiations and compromises. Obama is not negotiating in regard to Iran's nuclear ambitions. Negotiations with North Korea have stopped. No negotiations are being conducted with OPEC and Russia to increase oil output and reduce oil prices. Instead, green energies are being promoted, dumping the entire U.S. economy. High oil prices are the main reason for this looming double dip recession.

Obama cannot come along with Russia. He made concessions on nuclear warheads that will reduce America's defense power. Russia blocks any efforts to stop bloodshed in Syria and to hold accountable Iran for its nuclear ambitions. Russia cooperates with all U.S. adversaries. It was anticipated that Russia would enter the club of advanced democratic countries. Instead its political system has become autocratic. Any free speech or demonstrations are being suppressed and more and more people who exercise free speech are being jailed. Obama has not done anything to protect human rights in Russia, China, and other countries. China has taken over the U.S. domestic goods market because of its cheap products. It continued manipulating its currency that helped keep local products competitive. Obama has not done anything about it. As a member of the World Trade Organization, China was supposed to let its currency float freely.

U.S. foreign policy has to protect the country's interests and strengthen its national and economic security. Both are breached now. Young people have to understand that Obama had no experience on all these issues and has not learned much being in the White House. He skipped 60% of national security briefings. He was often out of office campaigning all the four years of his presidency. It might happen that he missed the briefing about security concerns about the U.S. Consulate in Benghazi, Libya.

Chapter 13
Liberalism

The country has two political parties and one is conservative (relies on original founding principles of the U.S. Constitution and society) and the other is liberal (in its policies, relies on everything that is happening today). Liberalism is about freedom and opportunities for citizens. However, the Democratic Party views liberalism differently, mixing it with modernist culture. They assume that the government has to extensively interfere in economic and social issues to alter the free market economy and take care of citizens by providing welfare. To do so, government constantly increases its spending for entitlement programs as European countries do.

The Obama administration's ideology is to establish social justice by providing support to those who earn less. Doing so, liberals represented by the Democratic Party drift away from core principles of capitalism that was the fundamental prerequisite for the liberalism reflected in the U.S. Constitution. The formula Capitalism + Liberalism = Individual Incentives made the U.S. a great country. However, it is in decline because of the ideology of modern liberalism adopted by the Democratic Party. Modern liberalism's ideology is to provide material support to more and more people in order to make them loyal to the party.

This ideology kills individual incentives in people to be self-sufficient by seeking opportunities and achieving goals. If you make health care free, people will be more secure and less motivated as in the United Kingdom (UK) or Canada. Less motivated people contribute to the society less and less. Why is the UK significantly less developed than Japan? People are heavily dependent on the government. They have every basic thing they need: free education, health care, and other entitlements. Why should they worry more?

The United States is catching up with its entitlement appeal: Social Security, Medicare, Medicaid, and now Obamacare. All this reduced individual motivation in the U.S. and the country's growth rates declined significantly. Liberals' promises are attractive to many. However, their policies are ruining this country. The growth rate in the first quarter of 2012 was 2.0% and in the second quarter was 1.3% only. If this trend holds, the country is heading to another recession. As soon as this number turns negative, there is a new recession in the country.

Chapter 14
Conservatism

Conservatism is about preserving traditions and origins of democracy and freedom and protecting Western civilization from modernist culture and totalitarianism. The more the government plays a role in economic and social affairs, the more it becomes autocratic and the more it restricts individual freedom and opportunity. Conservatism rejects this approach which is adopted by the liberals. Conservatism suggests deregulation (reduce rules and regulations so that businesses freely access loans, banks freely lend money, businesses freely sell their products and use their share of income for further growth) so that every individual has opportunities to succeed and achieve his or her dreams.

Conservatism is also for family and cultural traditions, rejecting the modernist approach to economy, life, family, and sexual orientation. The Republican Party is a conservative party and is for careful spending, free market economy, individual freedom and independence of individuals from government, self-reliance, traditional marriage, and pro-life values. The

Democratic Party is complete opposite of this. Therefore, its policies are not working and the economy is heading to a double-dip recession. America has lost about one trillion dollars because of slow recovery. The country is in decline.

Chapter 15
Waking up

President Obama is a nice man, husband, parent, and charming speaker, campaigner, and likable individual. However, these traits are not enough to be a good leader and competent president. He did not have any executive experience when he took office as President. He has not learned much being a President because there was no time to learn. Most of the time such inexperienced people get confused and cannot link events and developments.

Overwhelmed with the information flow, Obama was not able to digest all the details in economic, social, and foreign affairs. Confused and tired because of all this, he escaped - played endless rounds of golf, campaigned all the four years of his presidency, avoided most daily briefings on national security and other issues.

As voters, people hire the country's chief executive officer – the president of the United States who determines the country's direction. It may be a liberal or conservative direction. Liberals (Obama's administration) are committed to provide voters with whatever they can from the federal funds and are not able to control spending. Therefore, the national debt exceeds $16 trillion which is more than the country's annual gross domestic product (total market value of goods + services). Conservatives (Republicans) are committed to provide individual freedom and opportunity by making free market economy as it should be by reducing regulations, by making credit accessible to eligible borrowers. Under Obama even eligible borrowers cannot access credit.

The drawback of presidential elections is that the president is hired by mainly uninformed voters. Many of them do not understand fully what the candidates stand for. What experience they have and what they have achieved in their previous jobs. Obama did not have any executive experience whatsoever and holds the top executive position in the country. Is this not ironic? If a large corporation elects its Chief Executive Officer (CEO) by such methods, the corporation goes out of business very soon. Corporate CEOs are hired by corporate boards of directors which consist of professionals. They rarely make mistakes and do not have any right to do so because their stakeholders demand that they make right decisions.

In the case of hiring presidents, people hear their words and make decisions without checking the candidates' backgrounds. If a wrong individual is elected, the whole country suffers. Young voters who have a little life experience make their decisions based on what they hear or what they see: an attractive man who talks great and is likable. Remember, the hired president will impact your life not only for four years but beyond. Reaganomics created 40 million jobs, 25 million of which were created after President Reagan retired. The president's good and bad policies affect decades of your life. You are a college student, would you be able to find a good job if high-paying jobs are being eliminated? Now, fifty percent of college graduates cannot find jobs in their specialty. Obama is promising to keep interest rates for student loans low. Is this the only thing you want? If you do not get a good job, how will you repay this loan? Obama's policies, as you have learned, are not working and leading the country to the financial cliff.

When manufacturing is not here, there is no real economy that creates real value and there is no base for financial strength. Under Obama's economic policies, U.S. corporations exported at least two million jobs in four years. Obama's polices made capital flee from the country. Foreign direct investment by U.S. corporations was over $300 billion annually.

Voting is hiring the president whose policies may improve or worsen your life. Obama's policies worsened it. American families' median income has decreased by $4,300. Most of the jobs created during Obama's presidency were low-paying jobs. Poverty rates increased and one out of six Americans are below the poverty line. The number of food stamp recipients increased by 15 million over the last four years. In foreign countries, U.S. embassies are under attack. This scope of hostility was not seen since President Carter's times.

If you take funds out of the market in the form of taxes, the market will respond negatively and the economy slows down. If it does so, people will be laid off. They will not be able to pay their mortgages and produce little demand in the market. If demand decreases, the economy slows down more. Another recession will come along.

Young people, before voting, check each candidate's records in their previous jobs. Just wake up and learn about the candidates more before you make your vital decision.

CONCLUSION

In Part I of this book, I explained how our young people missed opportunity in 2008 to elect the right person as president. I also discussed Obama's soft hits in his economic, social, and foreign policies in Part II. To get reelected Obama made a series of cheap shots and I discussed them in Part III. Finally, I made suggestions for how to wake up and save America. The main solution is to elect a president who has solid experience in government, business, and community relations. If Romney has experience in all of them, Obama has experience in one – community work. He has little clue about how the office of the U.S. President works. He is overwhelmed and confused. By voting, you elect a president who may make your future life prosperous or ruin it. Be aware that you do not have a right to make a mistake. Do not be sold out for cheap shots or short-term benefits. Make a measured and wise decision.

Romney is offering himself to help you achieve your goals and aspirations, to remove bumps on your road, eliminating excessive governmental regulations and intervention. Remember that you can have a fair shot through market economy and more opportunities that Republicans promise. You do not have opportunities under a massive governmental takeover of industries and your freedom. It is always true that the more people have a fair shot (good jobs), the more people contribute their fair share (taxes) and the country and society prosper. Obama's concept of giving a fair share (welfare) to those who can work and earn and support themselves is a big mistake and a socialist theory. The world has seen it and it did not work in 29 countries emerging from communism. This idea is being implemented and the country has a tremendous amount of debt.

Taxing the rich more takes away money from them that could be used to reinvest and create more jobs. Higher taxes make the rich offshore their capital more and create businesses and jobs in other countries like China. From high taxation, capital flees. You cannot keep money of the rich in the country if you are going to take it away from them. They make their own decisions. This is the Obama way of pseudo-capitalism: to tax more, generate more in the government's treasures and redistribute more. This kills incentives to succeed as it happened in the former communist countries. Obama is not thinking about broadening the taxpayer base. His arithmetic is simple: tax the rich and redistribute the collected tax revenues. Because of this policy, the money of the rich may dry up one day and there will be nothing to collect and redistribute. Manufacturing will move out of the country. If there is no manufacturing in the country, there is no real economy that creates wealth, part of which is redistributed by the government anyway.

The alternative is the Romney way of modern capitalism; reduce taxes across the board by 20%, eliminate deductions and loopholes for the rich, broaden the tax-payer base and balance the budget. The tax reduction is a powerful incentive that attracts domestic and foreign investors in the U.S. Rapid economic growth will increase tax revenues dramatically and that will help reduce deficit and debt. The country's credit rating will improve and interest rates for credit will decrease. Prosperity to every individual will come from good jobs and hard work. If the rich prosper, others prosper.

If you do not have clear understanding of politics and vote blindly, you provide a bad service to yourself, siblings, parents, grandparents, kids, other relatives, friends, the society, and country. America will be in decline and your American dream will not come true. Wake up and make a wise decision. If you are not sure and may make a big mistake, stay home and do not participate in this serious decision making process.

I hope this book helped you learn much about the young generation's bad decision to elect Obama as president, President Obama's failed policies, and cheap shots, and some of my suggestions for how to fix the country by making a wise decision in the presidential election.